STYLE on a shoestring

ANNE McKEVITT & SHELLEY WARRINGTON

special photography by **COLIN POOLE**

STYLE on a shoestring

how to create fantastic rooms quickly and easily

Quadrille

DEDICATIONS

to **Don** *for being there*

My Mum **Jenny** *for never doubting me*

Aunt **Ethel** *for inspiring me. Sadly no longer with us*

My Mum **Jan** *for her belief and encouragement*

Publishing Director: **ANNE FURNISS**

Art Director: **MARY EVANS**

Design: **BALLEY DESIGN ASSOCIATES**

SIMON BALLEY & JOANNA HILL

Picture Research: **NADINE BAZAR**

Anne McKevitt's Assistant: **KES JAMES**

Production Director: **VINCENT SMITH**

First published in 1997 by

Quadrille Publishing Ltd

Alhambra House

27-31 Charing Cross Road

London WC2H 0LS

This paperback edition first published in 1999

Cataloguing in Publication Data: a catalogue record for this book is available from the British Library.

ISBN 1 902757 37 8

Printed in Hong Kong

contents

TO STYLE ON A SHOESTRING. COME IN, MAKE YOURSELF AT HOME AND LEAVE ALL YOUR PREVIOUS THOUGHTS ABOUT DECORATING OUTSIDE IN THE COLD. WE WANT TO DISPEL THE MYTH THAT TO HAVE A STYLISH HOME YOU NEED TO BE RICH. WE HAVE ALL BEEN LED TO BELIEVE THAT THE MORE YOU SPEND ON A PRODUCT THE BETTER IT IS, BUT THIS IS NOT NECESSARILY THE CASE. DON'T BE CONNED INTO THINKING THAT EXPENSIVE IS BEST. SOMETIMES, THE DIFFERENCE BETWEEN BASIC PAINT AND EXPENSIVE SPECIAL-EFFECT PAINT IS ONLY ONE MAGIC INGREDIENT – WATER! THE SAME GOES FOR A COSTLY KITCHEN AND A LESS EXPENSIVE ONE. THE

NTROD

DIFFERENCE IS OFTEN NOTHING MORE THAN FANCY HANDLES OR AN EXTRA-SPECIAL WORKTOP. WE WILL SHOW YOU IN THIS BOOK HOW TO ACHIEVE STYLE ON A SHOESTRING.

THE BOOK TACKLES ALL ASPECTS OF HOME DECORATING AND WE WANT YOU TO FEEL FREE TO EXPERIMENT AND HAVE FUN. START WITH SOMETHING AS SIMPLE AS A LAMPSHADE OR TURN AN OLD DOOR INTO A STYLISH DINING TABLE, CREATE AN INSTANT FOUR-POSTER BED, TRANSFORM A STAIRCASE OR TURN YOUR BATHROOM INTO A FANTASY DREAM WORLD. IF YOU'VE NEVER DONE UP ANYTHING BEFORE THERE'S NO NEED TO WORRY. WE'LL GIVE YOU THE CONFIDENCE, WITH EASY-TO-FOLLOW PHOTOGRAPHS, STEP-BY-STEPS, SIMPLE TEXT AND READILY AVAILABLE MATERIALS. WE'VE MADE LOADS OF MISTAKES IN THE PAST BUT YOU DON'T NEED TO: THIS BOOK IS PACKED FULL OF THE LESSONS WE HAVE LEARNT.

I HAVE A PASSION FOR COLOUR. I LIVE AND WORK WITH COLOURS INSPIRED BY NATURE: SKY BLUE, SUNNY YELLOW,

FOREST GREEN. THESE ARE THE OPPOSITE OF THE GREY SKIES, GREY SEAS AND LONG DARK NIGHTS THAT I GREW UP WITH IN THURSO ON THE NORTHERNMOST TIP OF SCOTLAND.

I ONLY HAD £150 AND LOADS OF VERY INEXPENSIVE IDEAS WITH WHICH TO DO UP MY FIRST FLAT. FRIENDS STARTED ASKING ME FOR TIPS ON DECORATING AND, THOUGH SELF-TAUGHT, I SOON HAD A LARGE NUMBER OF CLIENTS. I BELIEVE THAT IT'S IMAGINATION AND DARING THAT MAKE WONDERFUL INTERIORS AND I'M ON A CRUSADE TO RID THE WORLD OF FRILLS, FLOUNCES AND THE COLOUR MAGNOLIA!

UCTION

I HAVE PUT THIS BOOK TOGETHER WITH AN AUSTRALIAN FRIEND, SHELLEY WARRINGTON. WE MET WHEN WE WERE BOTH WORKING IN THE FASHION AND BEAUTY INDUSTRY. OVER DINNER ONE NIGHT, WE BEGAN DISCUSSING THE IMPACT MY DESIGNS HAD ON FRIENDS AND CLIENTS AND HOW WONDERFUL IT WOULD BE TO SHARE ALL OF THESE IDEAS WITH A WIDER AUDIENCE. THE IDEA FOR *STYLE ON A SHOESTRING* EVOLVED THAT EVENING AND QUICKLY BECAME THE BOOK THAT IS IN YOUR HANDS TODAY.

IT'S ALL UP TO YOU NOW. YOU DON'T NEED TRIAL AND ERROR, YOU JUST NEED TO TRY. MAKE COLOUR IMPORTANT, AND REMEMBER THAT MONEY IS NOT. ROLL UP YOUR SLEEVES, PICK UP A PAINT BRUSH, DYE A CUSHION COVER, WAKE UP YOUR HOME AND MAKE IT FANTASTIC. IT'S AS SIMPLE AS THAT.

inspiration

living areas

Take a fresh look at your living room, imagine you've never seen it before and look closely at all the furniture, knick-knacks and clutter. What really belongs here? You don't need to buy anything new, just throw out what you no longer like, and customise what you can't do without.

living with colour

Think of colours that make you happy: blue skies, yellow sunshine, orange sunsets, green forests. Now think of a scheme for your living room. You can use colour to change the atmosphere of your room. The enormous range of paints can be intimidating, but don't let choice scare you into choosing magnolia or off-white. Drab colours are no cheaper than bold ones.

A bold colour scheme doesn't always mean colour everywhere. Even small amounts of lime and purple make this room bright and colourful.

You can transform an old or second-hand armchair with felt and a length of rope.

You don't need a whole tin to paint one shelf, get cheap sample paint pots. An alcove can be transformed into a rainbow for less than the cost of a vase.

These glass doors were livened up using inexpensive sheets of coloured tissue paper stuck to clear glass with PVA glue. The bold effect makes even the hot pink walls and yellow floor look pale.

Mark out a square on your coffee table with masking tape and paint it. Remove the tape and add freehand brush strokes to the outer edges.

Your choice of colours need not force you to create a certain style. The same colour and similar tones can be used for both a modern and a more classic design.

If you want to rejuvenate a sofa but can't afford upholstery, use a dust sheet. Decorators' shops sell 100% cotton dust sheets in cream or white, but with one pack of fabric dye you can dye them in the washing machine. The fringing can be stitched on later.

In this room, the door and staircase take centre stage. If you let one or two big ideas lead a design, the rest of the room should follow.

Use bold furniture and brightly coloured tissue paper, stuck to the wall with water-based PVA glue, to contrast with cream walls and stripped pine floors.

coming up daisies

Changing the colour of your sofa is really no more difficult than changing the colour of your walls. This cheap, fun idea began with a dust sheet, a pack of fabric dye, one kilo of salt and felt for making daisies. Once you get used to the idea that you can't crush the flowers by sitting on them, you won't want to sit anywhere else.

(2) Cut the templates from the photocopy.

(3) Use a pencil to draw round the templates onto felt, then cut out the shapes. You need one full daisy for every cushion and a pile of leaves.

(4) Use bold, coloured wool to stitch the felt daisies to the cushions. Large hem stitches are simple to sew, and the stitches don't need to be perfect or even.

① You can photocopy this daisy design to create your own template. You will also need to draw out a simple leaf shape.

TOP TIPS

- Not only are dust sheets the right size for covering a small sofa, they also come ready hemmed, so there is no need to get out the sewing machine.
- Felt is the perfect material for cut-out shapes, as it never frays.

⑤ Lastly, stitch the leaves to the dust sheet. The bolder your choice of wool, the more impressive your sewing will look.

two in a box

Most modern living rooms need to be multi-functional. This tiny space acts as living room, dining room and playroom for a single mother and her daughter. Clever ideas were needed to provide storage and workspace without making it cluttered.

An unused fireplace can be transformed into a cupboard. If you want flames, just paint them on afterwards.

A fold-down table can double as a desk or dining table, then fold flat against the wall when space becomes a priority.

A sofa can become a sofabed, and sleeping bags can be used as throws.

Glue artificial flowers onto a plain blind for a different outlook.

stripped out and stunning

Dual-purpose living rooms can be given more than one design. Make your dining space feel different from your sitting space with paint and imagination. The more space you have, the more opportunity there is for creating fun effects.

You can create your own wavy wall from strips of timber cut to height at the builders' merchants. There is no need to call in a builder, just draw a curve along the ceiling and hang the wood from the ceiling with cup hooks.

BEFORE

This Jackson Pollock-style 'splattered paint' rug is fun and simple.

This ceiling rose is painted on freehand, but you could use a pattern or even a stencil.

Recycled bottles and a bike wheel make an excellent cheap light fitting.

Why should chairs always be floor-bound?

The haphazard roller strokes justify the off-balance empty picture frame.

Try this striking animal print stencil (see page 126 for suppliers).

Muslin draped over tall chairs instantly creates a theatrical dining room.

new for old

Before you dash out and spend money you don't have on furniture you don't need, think about how you can transform the possessions you already own, and make the old look new.

Get rid of bookcase

In this room the collections of art were brought together so they stood out, tongue-and-groove flooring was fitted to show off the rug and the sofa was brought up-to-date simply by fitting it with feet.

Finish with bold rug

Wall lights instead of ceiling light

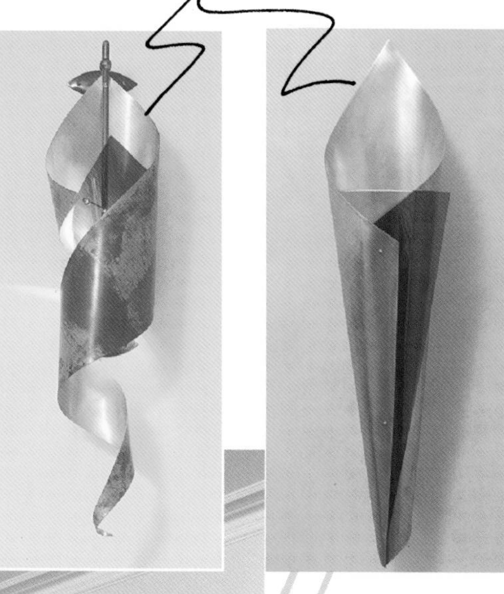

The fireplace was stripped, raised 40cm and surrounded with a concrete frame. This is a job for a builder, but with no need to decorate a mantelpiece or above the fireplace, you could save money.

Warm up Wall Colour

Raise fire + put in gas log fire

Put down beech floor instead of Carpet

Put legs on sofa to up date

painted masterpiece

This room shows what can be achieved on a shoestring budget. Paint was the only new purchase in the whole transformation.

Mark out squares with masking tape and paint with a colourwash. The leaf patterns are all stencilled (see page 126). The effect looks terrific, costs almost nothing and, once you have gathered the full range of colours needed, takes only a few hours.

ORE

Removing a door from a cupboard will force you to sort out the hidden clutter.

Fling out the flounce and breathe new life into old curtains, simply by hanging them properly.

A large floor needs a centrepiece, so if you can't afford a rug, paint your own.

The woodstain on this fireplace looked terrible and a coat of paint was the only solution. Use black paint on the tiles inside the fireplace to create an illusion of depth, and clear the clutter from the mantelpiece.

BEFORE

roll out a rug

If you are fed up with rugs rucking up under your feet, you can always paint your own. First, sand your floorboards, taking special care to vacuum up sawdust, otherwise it will settle on the paint. Then slap on a coat of primer and, once this is dry, a base colour of your choice.

(1) Draw out your design in pencil.

(2) You can get perfect straight lines with masking tape.

3 Stop paint seeping under the tape by running your finger firmly along each strip, to seal the tape to the floor.

TOP TIPS

- Don't cut corners with varnish. The more coats you use, the longer the design will last.

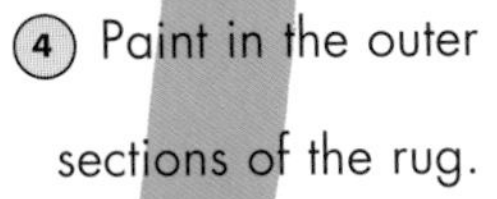

4 Paint in the outer sections of the rug.

5 Leave to dry, remove and replace the masking tape so you don't ruin the painting you have already completed, then paint in the central section.

6 Freehand designs and sponge print patterns will bring your rug to life. Finally, varnish with eight coats of acrylic matt varnish.

fantasy floors

Lurking under the carpet you probably have floorboards. They might look dreary when first uncovered, but a lick of paint and a bit of imagination can turn even the most grimy floor into a personal work of art.

This elegant parquet floor looks stunning with the blue colourwash over it.

TOP TIPS

- Always start painting at the wall furthest from the door and paint your way out of a room. Waiting for paint to dry from an island in the middle of your living room will take all the pride out of your achievement.

This floor has been made out of painted blockboard cut into triangles and fitted. It's a cheap idea that would work especially well in basements, where proper floorboards are rare, carpet too expensive and tiles too cold.

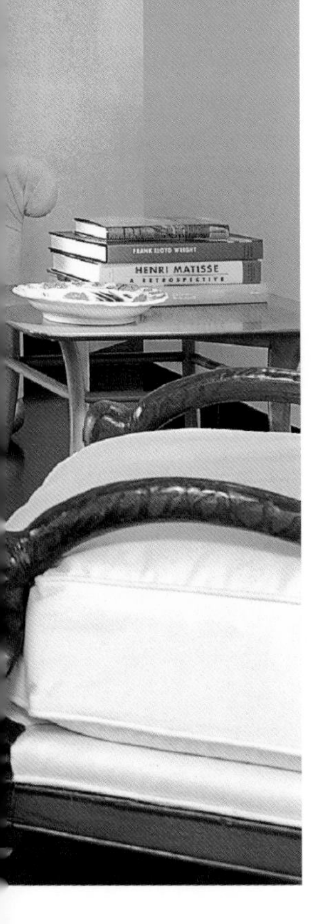

Stencilled patterns make excellent floor designs.

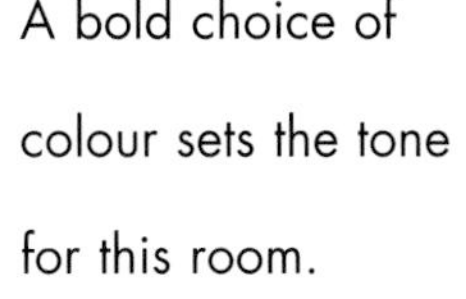

A bold choice of colour sets the tone for this room.

door dining

Dining room tables can cost a fortune and even the simplest and least attractive table top can set you back several hundred pounds. Doors, however, can be turned into unique designer tables for less than the cost of the dinner served on them.

Panelled doors are excellent for displaying small objects, like these keys. You can also stencil keyholes onto your walls and glue photocopies of antique keys to the wall above the dado rail.

If you can draw, then turn your table into a canvas. If not, cut pictures out of books or magazines and stick them on with PVA glue. Just remember, the more coats of varnish you apply the longer your artwork will last.

a cut above the rest

This design uses nothing more expensive than paint and coloured paper. The table legs are made from inexpensive wood dowelling cut to length at any builders' merchants.

(1) Give the door a coat of acrylic primer, then apply two coats of matt emulsion in a bold colour.

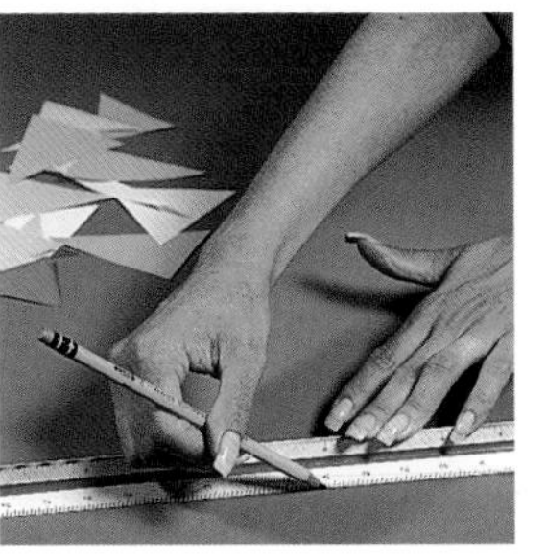

(2) Mark a 10cm border round the edge of the table.

TOP TIPS

- Instead of coloured paper use photographs, foreign money, magazine covers, playing cards, colour photocopies, prints, maps, comics, postcards, old birthday cards or tissue paper.
- If you're not sure you want a whole table in this design try it out with a placemat or tray.

(3) Cut up as many triangles of coloured paper as you need to cover the table top. This design uses six colours, but the table still gives an impression of being mainly purple with a bright pattern.

(4) Stick the triangles to the table with water-based PVA glue. Use straight edges along the border, then fill in the centre.

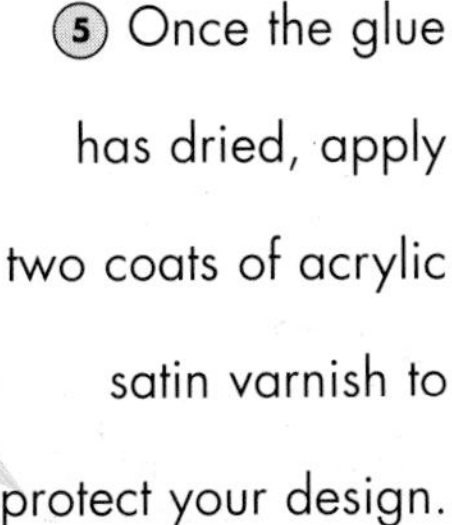

(5) Once the glue has dried, apply two coats of acrylic satin varnish to protect your design.

piano piece

This solid-looking table is made from a thin sheet of plywood cut to the shape of a piano and painted black. Add an edge to the thin top to give depth by bending a second sheet of wood around the piano shape.

The keyboard design can be used to enhance an ordinary rectangular table. Photocopy and use along one side of the table.

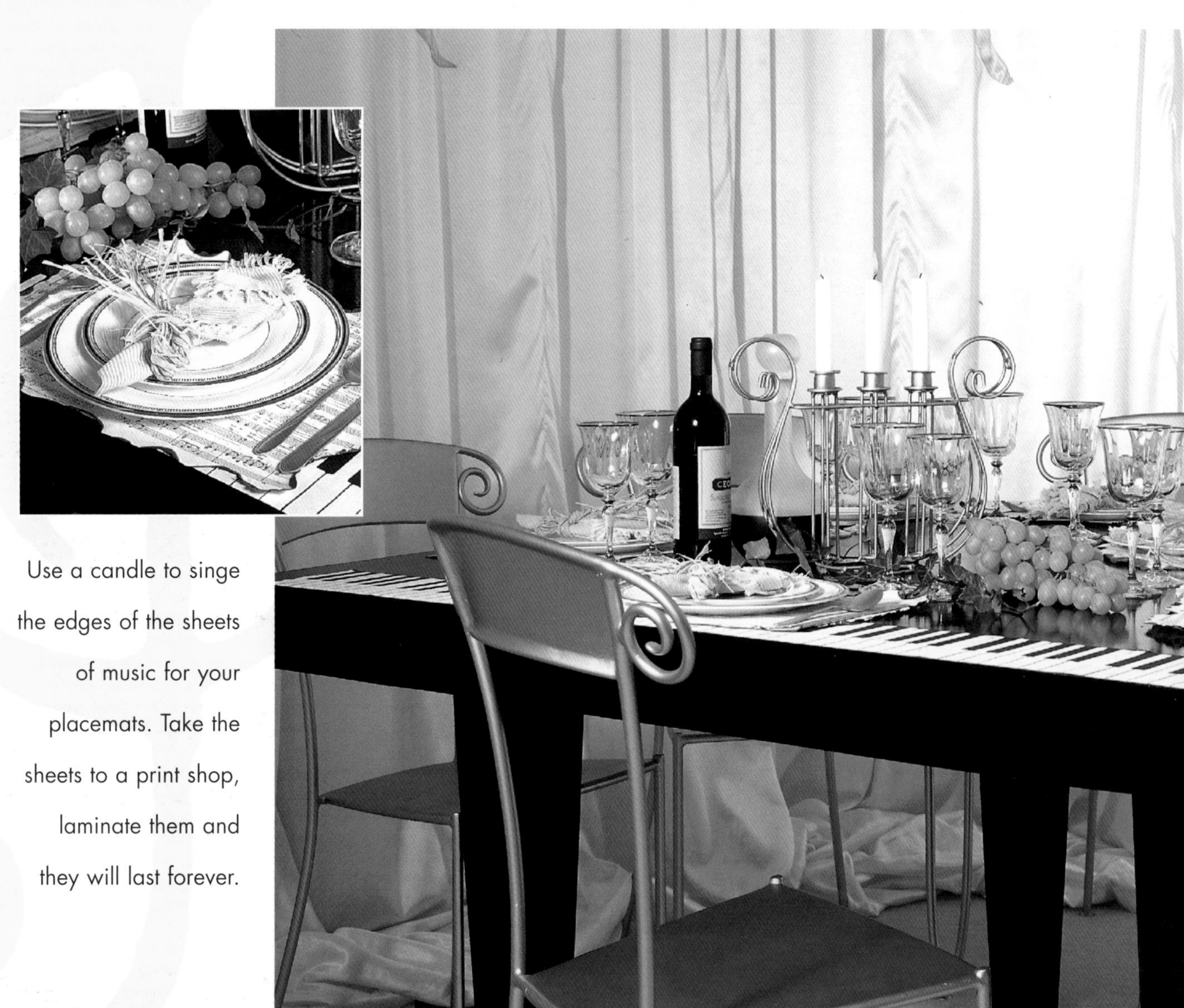

Use a candle to singe the edges of the sheets of music for your placemats. Take the sheets to a print shop, laminate them and they will last forever.

You can use this keyboard template for your own table top. You will probably need to enlarge this design to the right size as you photocopy it. Once you have enough sheets to cover one side of your table use PVA glue to stick the paper to the table, leave to dry and finish with four coats of gloss acrylic varnish.

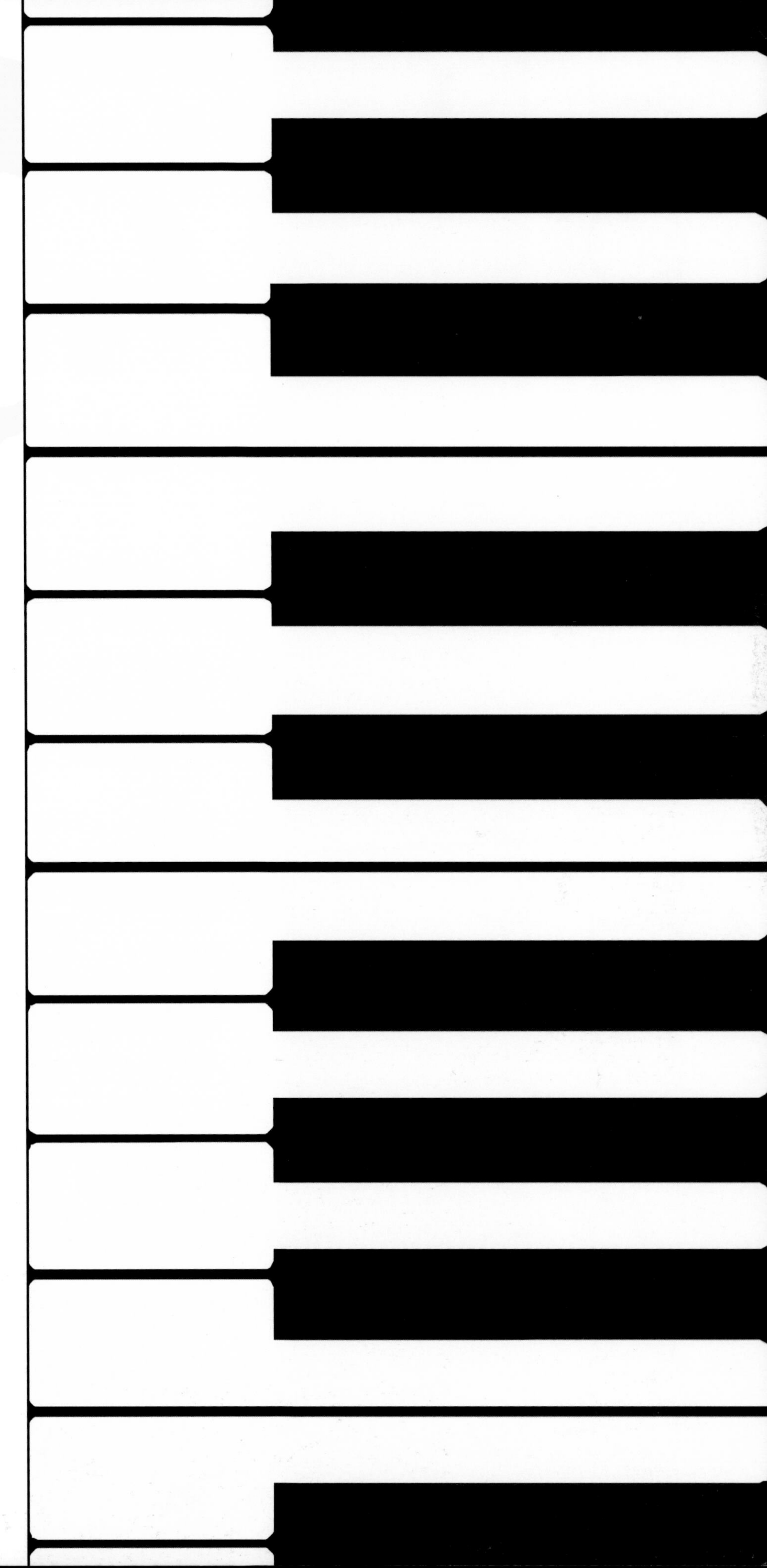

inspiration

kitchens

Kitchens must be hard working, but you may also want to eat and relax there. Think first about how you cook and where you will eat, as well as who helps with the cooking and keeps you company at the table, then design your kitchen.

clever curves

This was once a narrow, dead-end kitchen with no window. Install daylight bulbs on a time switch behind a wall of glass bricks to flood your kitchen with daylight, just during daylight hours. You can also cut diamond-shaped holes in your kitchen wall to let in extra light. Use a curved worktop to transform a once useless corner into valuable preparation space.

This floor mosaic made from broken tiles adds texture to the flat clean surfaces elsewhere in the room.

If you have always dreamed of a space-age kitchen, then think metallic. This kitchen looks modern and stylish, without feeling clinical, through the clever use of curved lines. Mixing straight and curved lines adds interest to a room.

TOP TIPS

- A breakfast bar is a wonderful way of adding to your preparation space.
- You could create the metallic look of this kitchen with silver spray paint.

A section of curved worktop can make your kitchen more interesting as well as giving you extra storage space.

kitchen creation

BEFOR

This entire kitchen has been created for £800. The secret is to buy a cheap self-assembly bottom-of-the-range kitchen pack and customise. The only other necessities are pots of paint and lots of imagination.

A stencil has been used to create the effect of a mosaic splashback. However, it is the final coat of varnish that really deceives the eye. Capture the glossy finish of a real mosaic with satin finish acrylic varnish; cover the rest of the wall with matt varnish.

Sand down the units to give the paint a 'key' to stick to. The heat and steam in a kitchen mean that you need to use oil-based paint on the unit doors. Use a small roller for a smooth professional finish.

TOP TIPS

- If the self-assembly kitchen pack comes with ordinary handles, change them to make your kitchen look plush.
- There's no need to refit a kitchen completely if it is just the existing doors you're unhappy with; paint them or get a carpenter to make new doors.

Tea towels make ideal covers for small cushions.

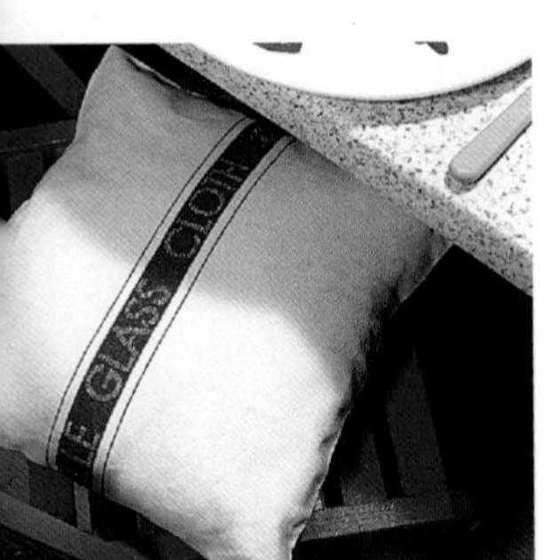

Use old utensils to create your own art. Glue-gun whisks, wooden spoons and a frame to the wall, then paint.

BEFORE

Use paint to bring an old fireplace up-to-date.

spoilt for choice

Most kitchen units are plain, but they can be made uniquely personal with a bit of daring. Don't go for run-of-the-mill splashbacks to protect your walls, be adventurous and use unusual materials.

Don't be afraid to use oversized handles on kitchen units. Textures and colours will always add interest to tiles.

Paint the doors and splashbacks in a light colour, then use masking tape to make two different widths and paint with a darker colour.

These units have been sprayed with metallic blue spray paint before sheets of stainless steel were stuck to the inside of the panels with specialist glue. A metallic silver spray paint splashback and large chrome handles all help to create a modern look.

Stretch builders' scrim across kitchen units and apply spray paint from a distance. When the paint is dry remove the scrim and you will be left with patterned cupboard doors. Wooden spoons can be screwed to the unit for handles. The splashback is painted corrugated plastic.

The white tile splashback has been sponged in rainbow colours using oil-based or tile paint. Do a freehand design on the doors for an individual touch.

Fit corrugated cardboard or plastic into the panels of ordinary units and paint with metallic copper paint. Stopcock taps make unusual handles.

£150 was all it cost to transform this kitchen into a sunny room. Bold yellows and bright oranges are especially good choices for painting kitchens with no natural light. Paint will brighten up cupboards, walls, floors and even the fridge.

BEFORE

You can laminate sheets of wrapping paper at a printing shop and fix them to kitchen units with wooden beading.

TOP TIPS

- Use a metal primer on the fridge before applying the top colour.

Corner tables take up virtually no space, yet they can transform the way you use a kitchen, or at least the way you eat breakfast.

Cheap shelves can be made from plywood and painted in a contrasting colour to the walls.

behind closed doors

Storage rules this kitchen, with units stretching from floor to ceiling. Think about storage as being either open, that is displayed on shelves, or closed, tucked away, in cupboards. Plates and glasses often look great on open shelves, but old pans are best kept out of sight.

BEFORE

A strip of marble set into the floor at an angle not only adds colour to the room, but more importantly it deceives the eye into believing that the room is wider than it actually is.

This kitchen is clean and uncluttered because all the storage features are hidden behind closed doors. Even the island work station houses a recycling centre for glass, paper, plastic and cans.

The stereo, the wine and the telephone all help to make the kitchen one of the most friendly rooms in the house.

Here, the shape of the island has provided inspiration for the pattern on the lino floor.

Get a carpenter to build an island work station in the middle of a large kitchen to provide work space and a focus for the design.

no space no waste

When estate agents say "open-plan kitchen", they often mean "poky kitchen and spoiled living room". Unless you want a messy compromise, decide how you can divide up your multipurpose space to give the impression that you have more room than truly exists.

In a small kitchen, you will need to be organised and keep clutter to a minimum. Think carefully about the available space and take time to plan your layout.

Here, the use of a banister rail, a raised floor and different flooring has created a cosy corner kitchen.

TOP TIPS

- Open-plan kitchens need strong extractor fans.
- Separate lighting for an open-plan kitchen will allow you to make the kitchen disappear at night when you are in your living space.
- The hob should be fitted into the worktop, allowing space on either side for a preparation area.
- If you find you are walking round your fridge to open it, then your door opens the wrong way. Most models are adaptable, so you can rehang the door by moving the hinges to the opposite side.

Don't imagine your kitchen will disappear if you choose units the same colour as the walls. It won't — you will just have a dull kitchen.

A solid storage unit with a front 30cm higher than the work surface has been fitted to keep prying eyes out of the kitchen. Because of this, mess can be left in and around the sink until you are ready to deal with it.

TOP TIPS

- Just because some items are fixed to a wall doesn't mean they cannot be removed. Be prepared to move or lose a radiator or air conditioning unit to free up wall space in a small kitchen.

spring clean

When your kitchen looks as bad as this one did and you have decided to get a new set of units, make the most of the opportunity to completely transform the room. It's not every year you buy a new kitchen.

BEFORE

While ordered storage makes the kitchen a pleasure to work in, imaginative details make the room a pleasure to look at. Zinc splashbacks are not expensive and plywood, cut into a wave design and stuck to the wall above the zinc, adds interest.

TOP TIPS

● Distinguish between the eating and preparation areas in a kitchen-cum-dining room by painting the floor in each space a different colour.

● Why boilers were ever left uncovered is a mystery. Of course you do need access and good ventilation, but cheap cupboard frontage and a lick of paint will remove the eyesore from sight.

A garden trellis makes an excellent gallery space for kids' paintings, held in position with clothes pegs.

BEFORE

Screw on fallen branches to make handles.

This tired kitchen table has been revamped with a coat of paint, a leaf print stencil and lashings of acrylic varnish.

inspiration

entrances

YOU HAVE TO FEEL SORRY FOR THE ENTRANCE; FOR TOO LONG IT HAS SIMPLY BEEN THE PLACE PEOPLE PASSED THROUGH ON THEIR WAY TO SOMEWHERE MORE INTERESTING. BUT THE ENTRANCE IS THE LAST PLACE YOU SEE AS YOU LEAVE HOME IN THE MORNING AND THE FIRST SPACE TO WELCOME YOU BACK AT THE END OF THE DAY, SO IT DESERVES SPECIAL TREATMENT.

spare change

We only had £40 to sort out this hallway. The hall had no less than nine doors leading from it, and so many doors painted one colour and the walls another created an eyesore. Painting from floor to ceiling with one colour camouflaged the doors and gave it a more uniform look.

BEFORE

Two coats of turquoise emulsion provided a really rich base colour. With an ordinary sponge, violet, mustard and white streaks of paint were smeared over everything. This is fun to do and will change your hallway into a room in its own right.

TOP TIPS

● When applying paint streaks, finish all the walls with one colour first, then allow this to dry before starting on the next colour. This will prevent different colours running into one another.

The paint came in under budget, by £2. If you find you have some spare change left over, why not varnish it to the floor for a joke and watch as your friends try to pick it up!

Be extravagant with a great mirror to complete your hallway.

go with the flow

Don't always think in straight lines. The introduction of curves to the wall, floor or stair treads in an entrance hall or passage will make the space more interesting and disguise what might otherwise be seen as a dull narrow area.

A curved rug in a hallway will stop you thinking of the entrance merely as the area at the bottom of the stairs. If you can't find a rug you like, design one yourself and take measurements and sketches to a carpet cutter.

Use bent copper piping to create an unusual hall-way light. An electrician will need to wire this for you.

Disguise an ugly radiator with a cover. This one takes its inspiration from the Manhattan skyline. Raid a chemistry set for individual test tube vases to hang above it.

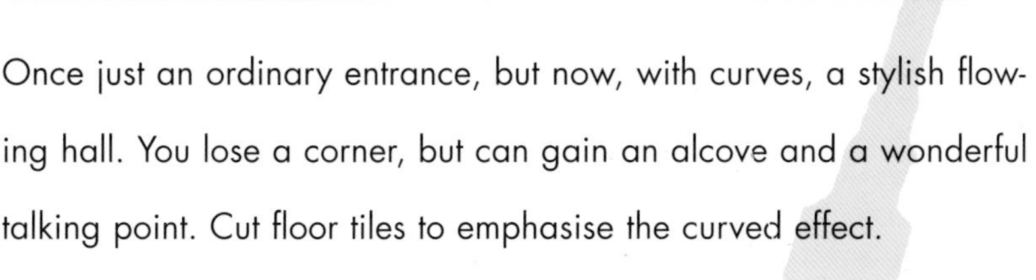

Once just an ordinary entrance, but now, with curves, a stylish flowing hall. You lose a corner, but can gain an alcove and a wonderful talking point. Cut floor tiles to emphasise the curved effect.

three-way stairway

A stairway is an opportunity to express your individuality. Think of a theme or design idea and go for it.

The African design was inspired by tribal carvings and uses earthy colours. The Calypso design began with the diamond-shaped border. Don't be afraid to decorate a large space with colours chosen to complement one small detail. The 1950s Hollywood design started with a can of gold spray paint, a great way to glamorise banisters, furniture or accessories.

CALYPSO

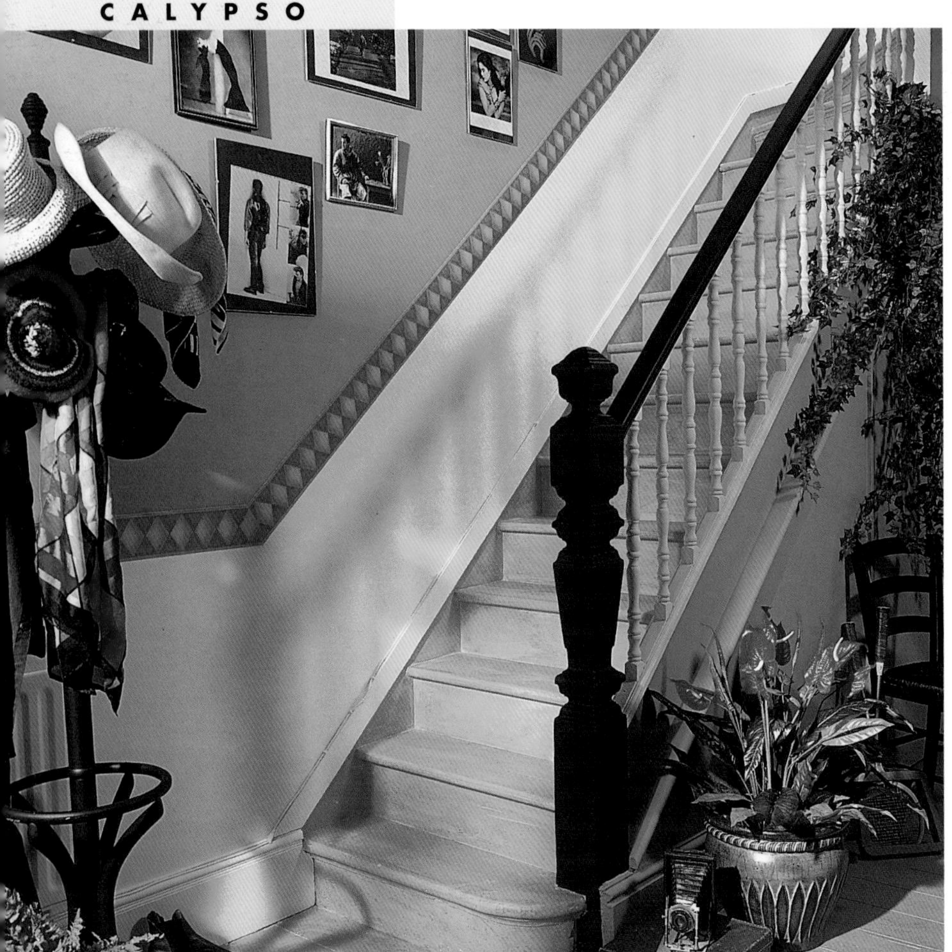

Hang small photographs or prints above a staircase; it is the best way to view them. Paint stairs and the floor with peach, then put on a scarlet colourwash and varnish.

You can find similar African designs in any library. Don't copy any design precisely, as this kind of art shouldn't be too exact.

Finger painting is an easy way to jazz up a stairway. Don't be afraid to add small patches of different colours, like this indigo blue.

AFRICAN

Stick torn strips of tissue paper to any wall with spray glue, then coat with matt varnish. Use a gold marker pen to write on the wall and, if your handwriting isn't great, get a friend to help you out. Paint a carpet runner on your stairs, use a stencilled design to cover the "runner" then protect with acrylic varnish.

HOLLYWOOD

outside inside

Niches exist only for decoration and display. Use a strong colour as a backdrop for favourite things, or try a paint effect to pick up on decorative ideas you are using elsewhere.

You could try floor tiles on your stairs. The cobalt blue looks striking with the contrasting earthy colours of terracotta and copper.

TOP TIPS

- Slate tiles look and feel great. They bring millions of years of earth history into your home. However, slate is very absorbent and needs to be sealed with wax every six months.

If you long for lush green pastures, you can buy moss from any florist and stick it to a radiator cover with PVA glue. Here, the radiator grille is made from ordinary garden trellis.

Fake ivy hung around the stairwell and decorative branches add to the outside-in effect.

inspiration

bathrooms

Bathrooms are about escape, a chance to pamper yourself and have some peace and quiet. Take a good look at your bathroom and customise, paint, tile or change it in any way you can imagine to make it more an expression of your personality.

flying high

Bathrooms can be themed more easily than larger rooms. Take one item you love, such as a print, painting or photograph, and use these colours and textures throughout the room.

Here, the walls have been colourwashed and strips of wood painted like the towels in the print.

SUN & SAND

If you paint radiators the same colour as the wall they will be less of an eyesore.

It's often cheaper to re-enamel your bath than to replace it.

Use sheets of wood to make a window surround, changing the shape of the window and making it a feature.

NEO-CLASSICAL

Real sandstone tiles look great, but are expensive. As ever, there is a cheaper way — colourwash. Lay wooden tiles and paint on a base coat of cream, then wash on a top coat of sandy coloured matt emulsion, followed by several coats of varnish.

TOP TIPS

- Not only are wooden tiles cheaper than stone, but they also feel warmer, especially on bare feet.
- When using paint to imitate sandstone, slate or marble, colourwash each wooden tile as a separate piece of stone. Don't let the paint overlap from one tile to another.

centuries apart

Decorating your bathroom needn't mean replacing the bathroom suite. You can achieve a Victorian mood or a modern feel by changing nothing more expensive than paint and wallpaper.

The rich deep colours make this bathroom feel majestic.

If you have a Victorian bath, you can make it unique by painting the exterior with oil-based paint.

The stencil pattern on the panels also sets this room firmly in the Victorian era.

Or you can treat the same space and accessories with different paint to make the room feel modern and airy. This colour scheme was chosen to complement the wallpaper border.

Stencilling tile shapes costs a fraction of the price of real tiles. Seal with many layers of acrylic varnish.

on the tiles

This bathroom began life as a cupboard. If your bathroom is too narrow for a bath yet you long for a soak, try a Japanese tub – ideal if you thought you only had space for a shower.

BEFORE

If you want to tile a curved surface, mosaic tiles are the perfect choice. Fix the mosaic sheets to the plywood with tile adhesive, then grout, just as you would ordinary tiles.

You will need a step to lead up to your Japanese tub. This is more costly, but improving or creating a new bathroom is one of the best ways to add value to your home.

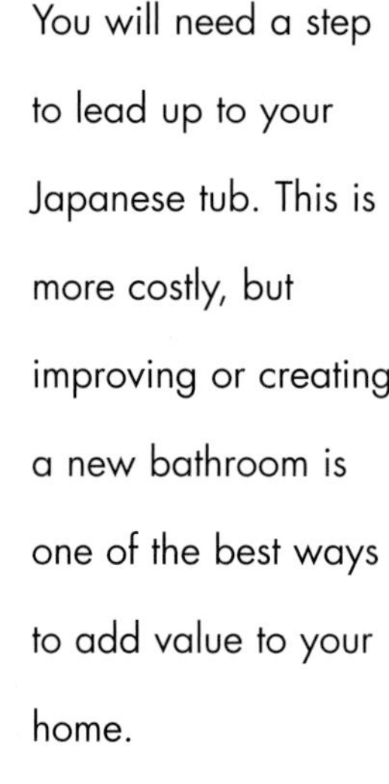

① Mosaics aren't always fiddly. The lazy way to perfect patterns is to use mosaic tiles, available in 30cm-square sheets.

② With ruler and pencil, draw your design onto the back of the sheet. Cut out using scissors.

TOP TIPS

- Sheets of mosaic tiles are sold with paper protecting the front of the tiles. Adhesive needs to go on the unprotected side.
- Use a damp sponge instead of a spatula to apply grout with.
- Add a border of mosaic tiles to your existing bathroom tiles.

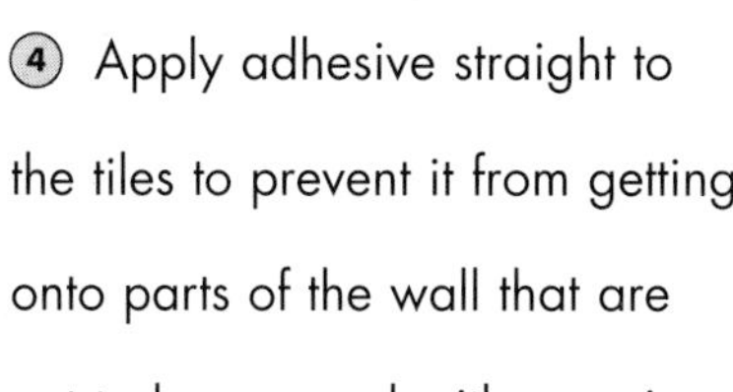

③ Check your design is correct before you fix the tiles to the wall.

④ Apply adhesive straight to the tiles to prevent it from getting onto parts of the wall that are not to be covered with mosaic.

⑤ Arrange the tiles on the wall and leave to dry for 24 hours.

⑥ Use a wet sponge to dampen the backing sheet then peel it away from the tiles.

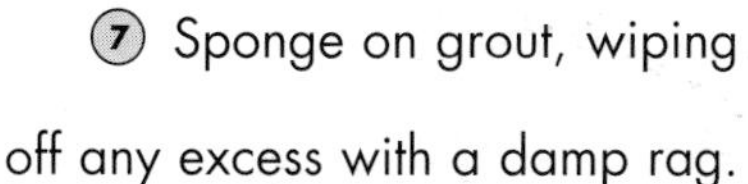

⑦ Sponge on grout, wiping off any excess with a damp rag.

making waves

Most people have chrome fittings and straight lines, so be different – have your bathroom fittings electroplated or use curves and wave shapes to make your bathroom special.

An electroplater can plate your existing bathroom fittings in any metal finish, such as copper. Ask for the plating to be sealed and you won't have to worry about tarnish. Pewter, brass, gold and brushed nickel all make excellent plating finishes.

This chic copper sheet has been curved to screen off the toilet area, making the bathroom more elegant.

Using a jigsaw, cut plywood into waves that can be stuck along the front and top of the bath. Create an ocean effect on the floor. Have large sheets of plywood cut into tiles and paint them with a turquoise and white colourwash, then varnish for protection.

stroke of genius

It's not essential to use tiles and water-resistant wallpaper in a bathroom. If you really want to give your bathroom a treat use inventive paint techniques.

① You can use bronze metallic paint as a base for a striking lattice design.

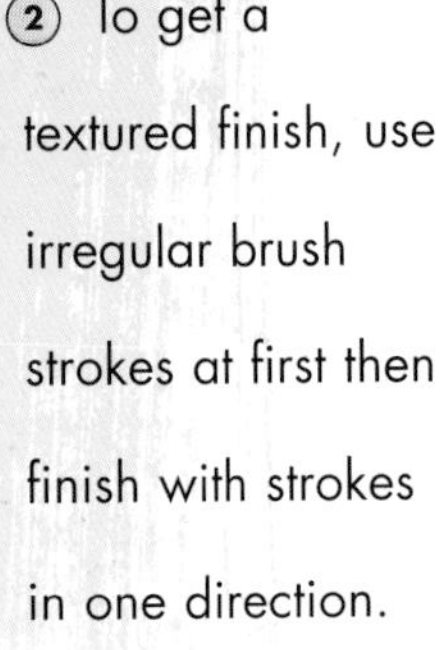

② To get a textured finish, use irregular brush strokes at first then finish with strokes in one direction.

TOP TIPS

- If you are using metallic paint make sure the room is well ventilated; open every window and door you can. You should also wear a face mask.
- It is advisable to use extra coats of acrylic varnish around the sink and bath.

③ Use matt emulsion paint to make irregular vertical and horizontal dashes across the wall. Slowly lift the brush from the wall as you reach the end of each stroke for a perfect effect.

④ Allow the first colour to dry, then repeat with the second and third colours.

Let your imagination run wild. A bold colour with a block-painted border in contrasting white looks striking.

BLOCKED

PILGRIM

CHEQUERBOARD

SCRUNCHED

To camouflage uneven wall surfaces, scrunch up a plastic shopping bag, dip it into a darker paint and press over the lighter-coloured base coat.

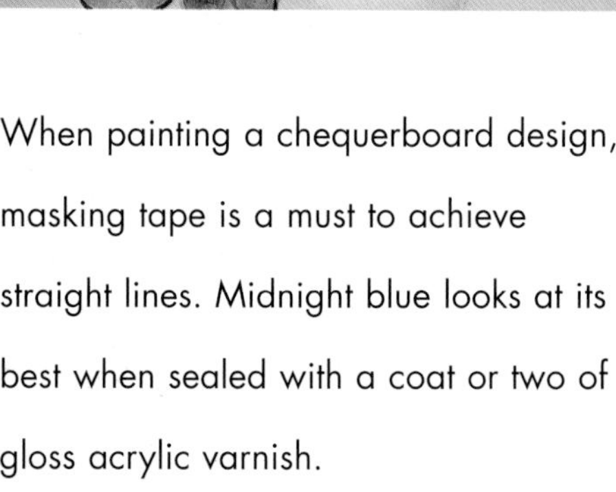

When painting a chequerboard design, masking tape is a must to achieve straight lines. Midnight blue looks at its best when sealed with a coat or two of gloss acrylic varnish.

MIDNIGHT BLUE

TISSUE

COLOURWASH

GILDED

YCHEDELIC

Unusual colours, shapes and materials like torn tissue paper will liven up any bathroom. Apply extra varnish to areas likely to get wet.

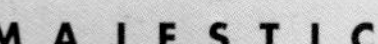

MAJESTIC

going overboard

A small bathroom is the ideal place to let your imagination run riot and follow through a theme. Go over the top with accessories like these toy sea creatures; be daring and try out colours that you wouldn't normally use; splash out on a great mirror and paint shapes on the floor.

Drape netting behind the mirror and entangle crabs, lobsters and fish in it to give the bathroom an undersea feel.

The wave-shaped cork splashback was cut with scissors and sealed with acrylic varnish.

If your bathroom looks timid and too small, paint it in bold colours and the room will stand out as if it were twice the size.

BEFORE

Glossy paint gave this bathroom an institutional look; with a change of colour and a less shiny finish it has been revitalised.

Hang your bits and bobs on a smart row of pegs.

Wrap a length of fake suede around the washbasin to hide the pedestal and create storage space.

inspiration

bedrooms

Bedrooms should be enticing, whether you want comfort, solitude or fun. We spend a third of our lives in bed, so it's worth taking time and making an effort to create a room in which you are happy to relax, restore your energy and wake up.

grand illusions

Too much white can feel clinical and cold, but use this colour well and it will look calm, simple and sophisticated.

The budget for transforming this room allowed only for paint and lining material. Furniture and a headboard painted the same colour as the sheets will pull the colour scheme together.

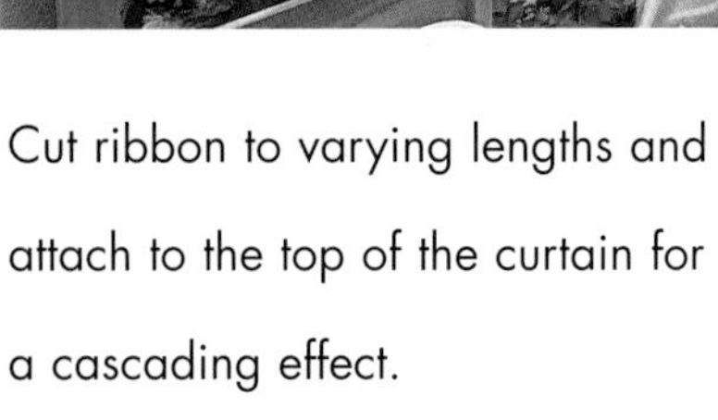

Cut ribbon to varying lengths and attach to the top of the curtain for a cascading effect.

Use gold chain hung from cup hooks in the ceiling to suspend the curtain pole in the air.

The secret of a striking black-and-white room is to use lots of black, but keep each bit small. The harlequin design, stripes and stencils all provide contrast in a white room without creating pools of darkness.

This hearth has been stencilled, a budget alternative to tiles. A touch of greenery will bring a black-and-white room to life.

the no-poster four-poster

The no-poster four-poster is one of the most elegant ways to turn a nap into true beauty sleep. It's cheap, simple and romantic without being too feminine. Once the rings are in place you can change the drapes as often as you fancy; try inexpensive muslin or dress lining for the summer, and velvet or brocade for cooler nights.

You need eight lengths of fabric for the drapes. Four lengths will drop from the ceiling to the floor and need to be a metre longer than the height of your room. Two other lengths each need to be one metre longer than the length of your bed, and the final two lengths should be a metre longer than the width of the bed.

Blanket boxes can be painted with crackle glaze and finished with a fleur-de-lys stencil.

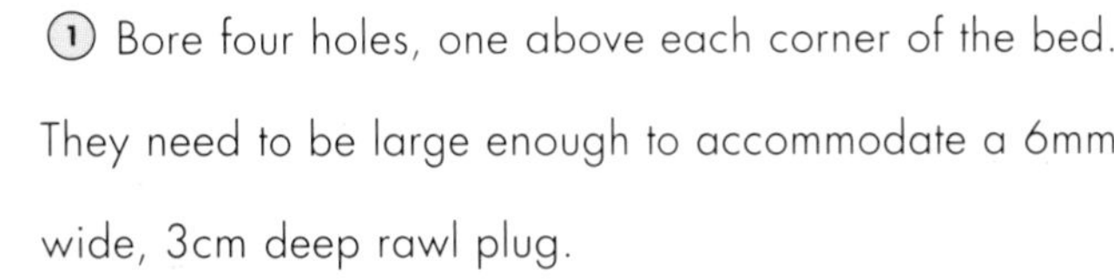

① Bore four holes, one above each corner of the bed. They need to be large enough to accommodate a 6mm wide, 3cm deep rawl plug.

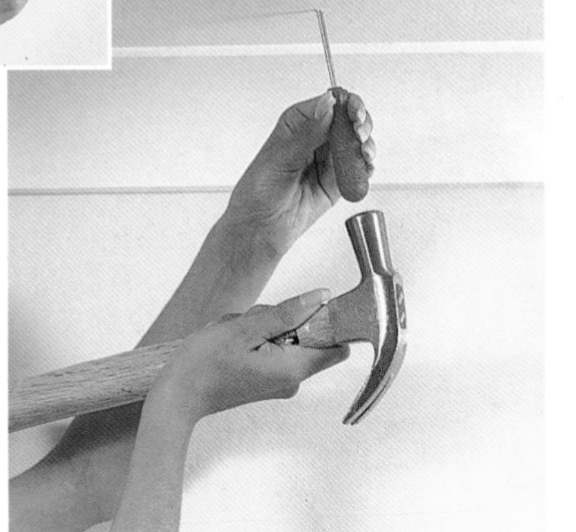

② Use a hammer and screwdriver to tap a rawl plug into each hole. Rawl plugs are vital as they provide a strong grip for the hooks and can support material.

③ Choose the size of the hook to fit the rawl plug and twist the hook up into the rawl plug until it fits snugly and won't go further without forcing.

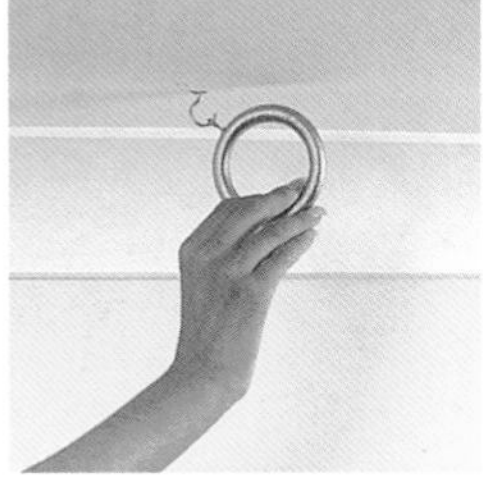

④ Fix a ring to each hook. If you want to hang bulky material, use a large ring.

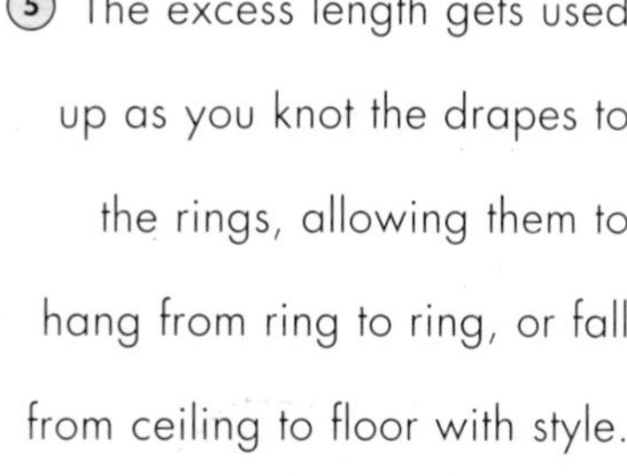

⑤ The excess length gets used up as you knot the drapes to the rings, allowing them to hang from ring to ring, or fall from ceiling to floor with style.

a touch of the unexpected

The temptation can be to play safe, but experimentation can really pay off, and the bedroom is a great place to try out ideas that are for your eyes only. These two rooms look sumptuous, yet the budgets from which they were created were modest.

The raspberry stripes and violet bedspread in this room look stunning and the transparent curtain hung from the curtain rail add to the romance. An inexpensive canopy kit draped with muslin will add panache to any bedroom.

A sheet of voile netting pierced with imitation flowers makes an unusual bedhead centrepiece for this room.

Use the colours of your bedspread to inspire your choice of flower.

out of the closet

Be creative about your use of space, and if there is a chance of conjuring an extra bedroom out of a cupboard, then wave that wand.

This was an internal cupboard with no natural light. To let in some light, one door was replaced with opaque glass that has a leaf motif etched into it. A large mirror maximises the available light and space.

BEFORE

Clever use of hanging storage and a fold-up futon provide extra floor space.

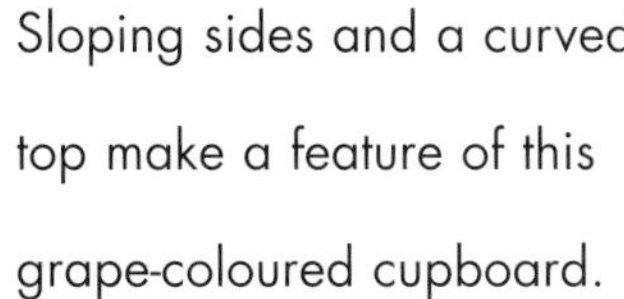

Sloping sides and a curved top make a feature of this grape-coloured cupboard.

The handles are cut from plywood and fixed to the cupboard doors with carpenter dowling and two screws.

Cupboards, and especially cupboard doors, need not be rectangular and dull. It is no more expensive to make a curvy door than a straight one.

baby steps

Please, please, please never paint your nursery in pastel shades. Babies can only see bold colours, the niceties of soft pink and 'baby' blue are lost on very young eyes. If you want a nursery to stimulate your child, use strong colours and reflective surfaces, preferably lots of them.

Babies spend many of their waking hours gazing at the ceiling. An expanse of white is not going to stimulate their curiosity.

Hang a wooden ring from cup hooks screwed to the ceiling then dangle flowers, bells and toys from it.

This shelving unit was once plain, dull and doorless. Ask a carpenter to cut and install doors to suit your design ideas. Use small sample pots of paint for lots of colour.

TOP TIPS

- Varnish the walls even if you have wallpaper – one coat and you need never worry about grubby little hands.

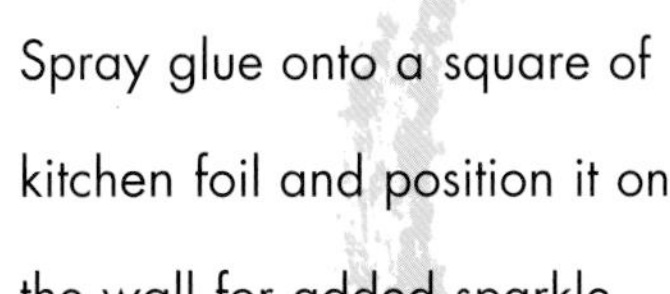

Spray glue onto a square of kitchen foil and position it on the wall for added sparkle.

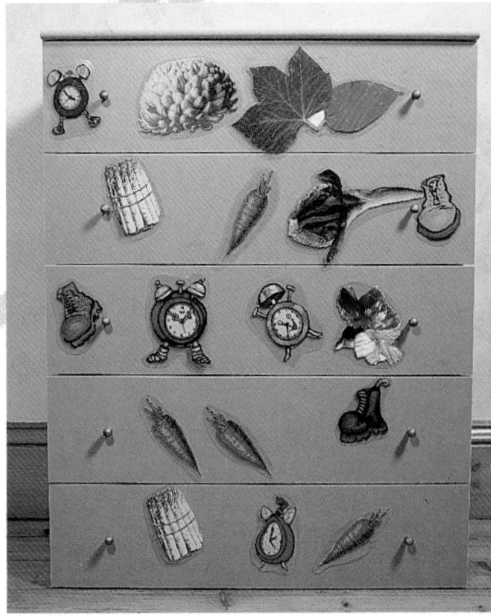

Velcro and laminated giftwrap is used so that children can move the cutouts around.

kids on the go

Don't waste money on expensive children's furniture that your kids will grow out of. Instead, buy standard furniture and adapt it as they get older. The must-have design of one year will be out-of-date twelve months later.

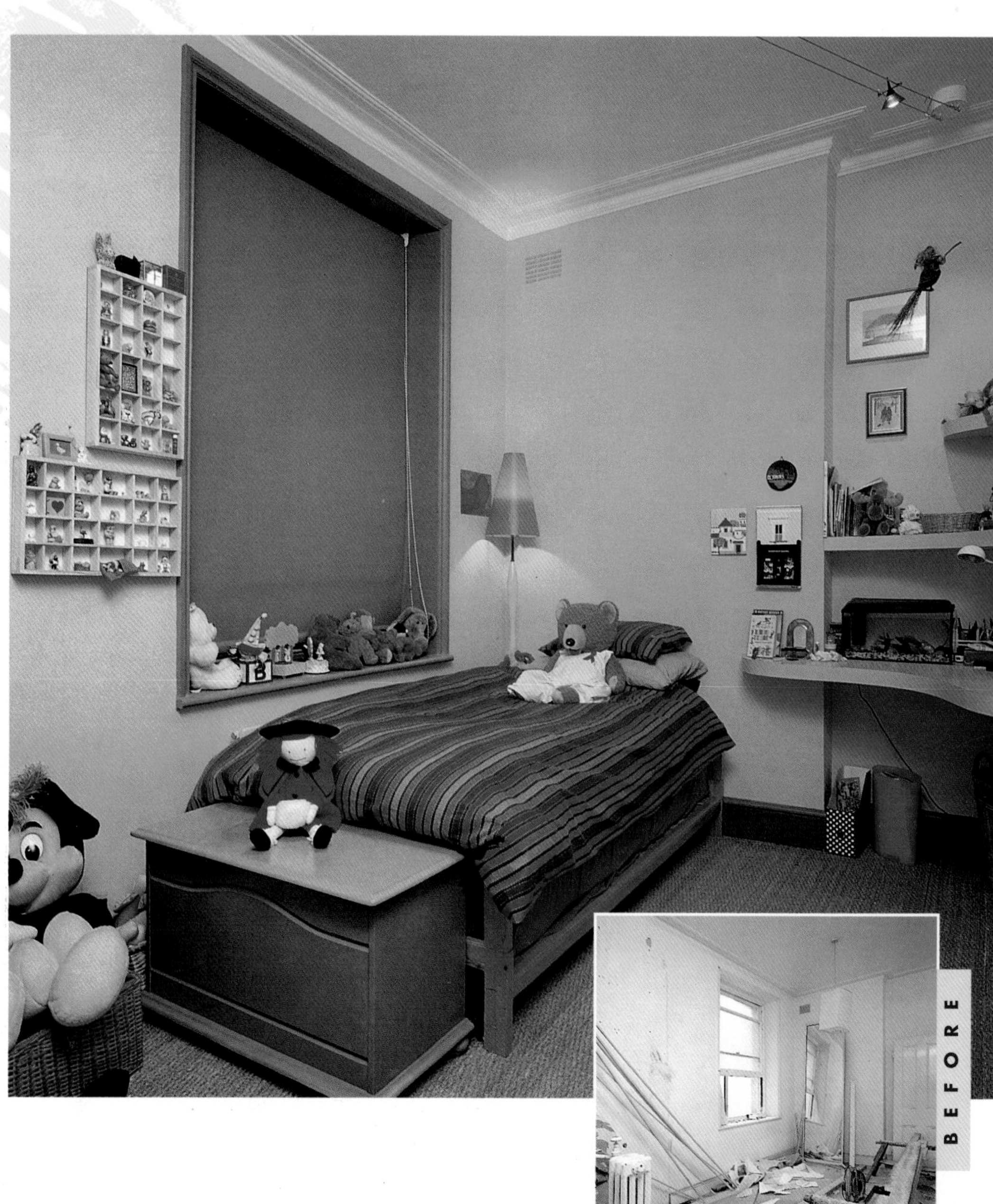

These shelves are fine for cuddly toys, but one day they will hopefully be used for files and textbooks. The bottom shelf is deep enough to use as a desk.

A teenager's bedroom is their own private domain, so let them make their own design choices.

TOP TIPS

● Make sure you have ample storage for a T.V., stereo and computer.

A tailors' dummy is a stylish option to drape clothes on rather than leaving a pile on the floor. A sari makes an excellent curtain and painting the inside of the shelving unit a different colour from the rest of the walls breaks up the lime colour.

jazz up your bedroom

This transformation cost £180. Thinking first about space and the use of a room is preferable to simply going out and spending money.

BEFORE

Make the best of those parts of a room you can't stand or change. The ugly, boxed-in fireplace was painted a very different colour from the walls and became the bedhead.

Make your own wardrobe surround from plywood and hang a cane blind for door. A colourful rug with a bold pattern will distract the eye from a dull, worn, carpet.

If you need a desk but haven't the space, try a folding kitchen table.

The window is dressed with strips of felt tied with ribbon.

BEFORE

The abstract design on the wall behind the bed was achieved using paint rollers of varying widths. This design was carried through to the bedspread using synthetic suede for a fashionable look.

Who needs handles with all these holes to pull? Update boring doors with holes cut with a jigsaw and backed with dyed muslin.

inspiration

chairs & things

A piece of furniture can often make or break the look of a room. Rather than spending money on a piece of production-line furniture, buy cheap or second-hand pieces and add your own touch of style.

lights, action

Lampshades are incredibly expensive for what is no more than a piece of fabric wrapped around a wire frame. Light stands also cost far more than they should. Buy a basic lampshade and base, then paint and stick on objects to create something special. If you need to, protect your work with a coat of matt acrylic varnish.

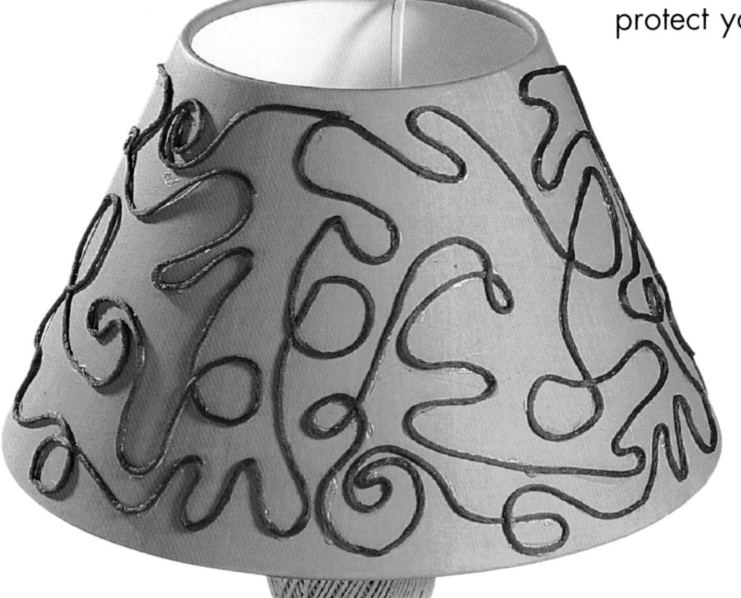

Once you have finished drawing a design on your shade you can use the felt-tip pens to decorate the base.

Balls of string have been slipped over the base and a pattern of string glued to the shade.

Raid the garden for design inspiration and wrap twigs around the lamp stand. The shade here is decorated with fake leaves.

① Use felt-tip pens to draw even stripes all round the lamp.

② Protect your work with one coat of matt acrylic varnish.

Stamps can be stuck to a shade with PVA glue.

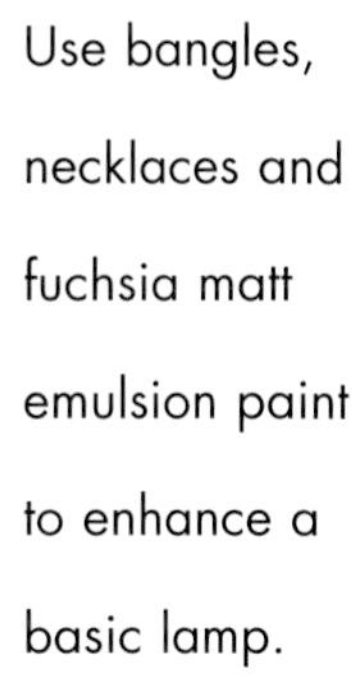

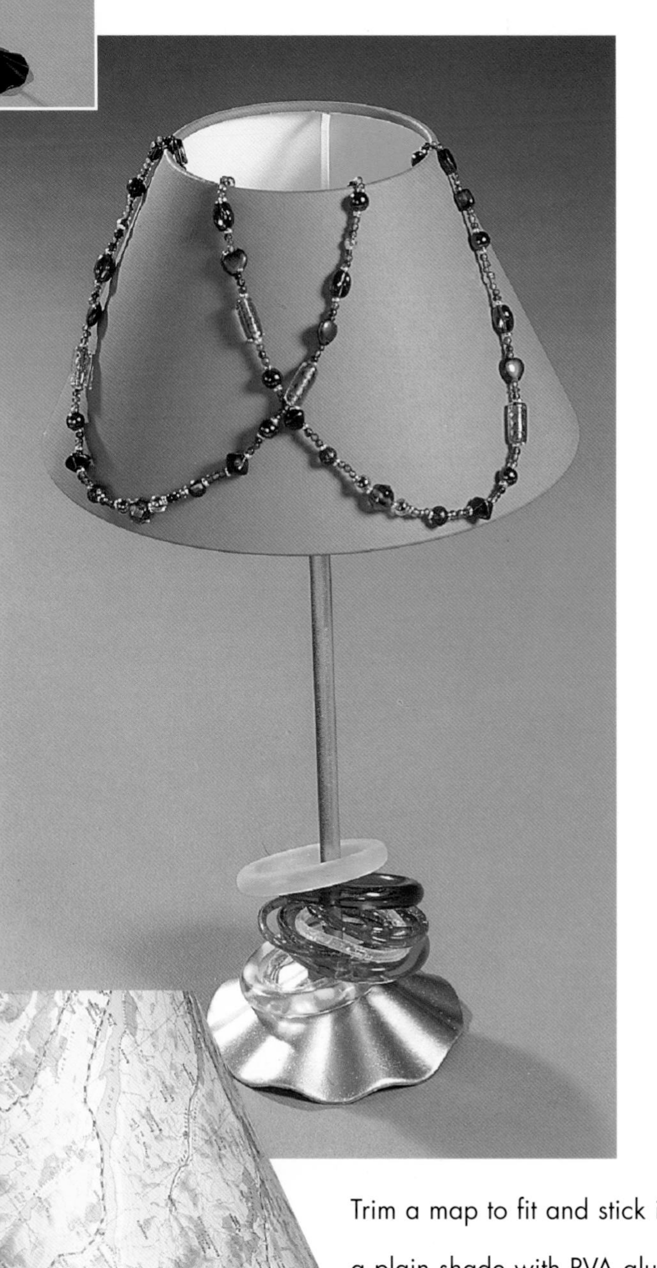

Use bangles, necklaces and fuchsia matt emulsion paint to enhance a basic lamp.

Stick-on appliqué, available from any dress fabric shop, is used on this design.

Trim a map to fit and stick it to a plain shade with PVA glue.

sitting pretty

For some reason the one seat guaranteed to be used every day is rarely decorated. The most popular seat in the house should be made to feel special, so why not draw a design freehand or stencil with matt emulsion or spray paint?

You will need to lightly sand a plain wooden seat with fine sandpaper to give the paint a surface to bond to. Varnish your design to protect it.

Shops offer a limited selection of towel rails, but it's amazing what you can do with some rope, copper piping, a ladder and some hose pipe.

Protect your towels from rust marks by sealing all metals with varnish.

chairs 'n' shelves

Second-hand chairs can be bought for a couple of pounds. Don't be put off by their colour or shabby condition. With a lick of paint and a piece of fabric you can breathe new life into any chair.

First choose a piece of fabric for the seat pad and then decide on a colour and design for the frame.

Junk chair seat pads tend to be old-fashioned, but they are very easy to update. Lift the cushion out of the chair, wrap material round it, tack or staple the fabric into position and, finally, trim off any excess fabric.

A chair of the past becomes a chair of the future with a coat of paint, 20m of ribbon and a silver seat pad.

TOP TIPS

- When looking at junk, keep an eye out for good shapes and solid construction. Avoid anything that creaks, rocks or has woodworm.
- If the seat pad on the chair you love is beyond repair, cut fireproof foam to shape and cover it.

FRUIT SALAD

AFTERNOON TEA

SOAP OPERA

SCHOOL'S OUT

Ugly mess belongs in cupboards, hidden from sight. Shelving, however, is storage on view. You should use your shelves as much for display as for storage. Make the most of this opportunity to show off your favourite things.

Decorating the front of your shelves with fake flowers, cake tins, nailbrushes, drawing pins, hessian and bottle tops gives the most dreary shelf a life of its own.

bookcase bonanza

A bookcase shouldn't just be restricted to housing books. Versatility is the name of the game. For under £20 a chipboard bookcase has to be the cheapest way to buy new furniture for any room in the house.

A painted cactus design and rope handles give this bookcase-turned-cupboard a Western feel. Terracotta pot feet add height and complete the design.

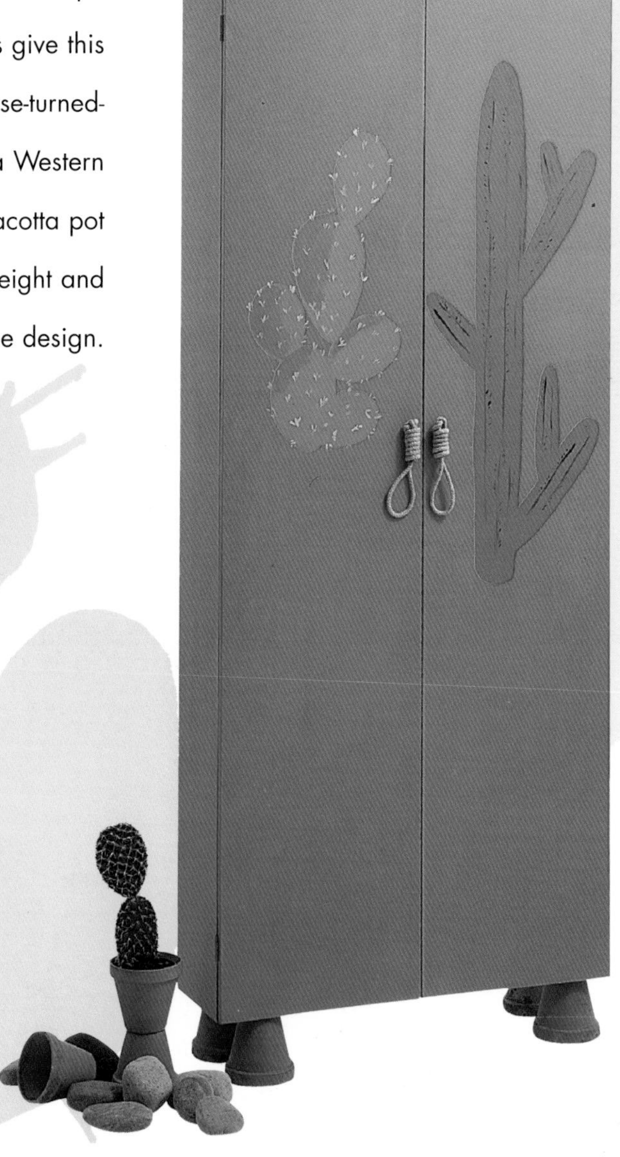

DIY superstores sell plaster cornicing, which can be added to the top of your bookcase. Dress fabric, cheaper than upholstery material, is an excellent way to cover the shelves of a kitchen cabinet.

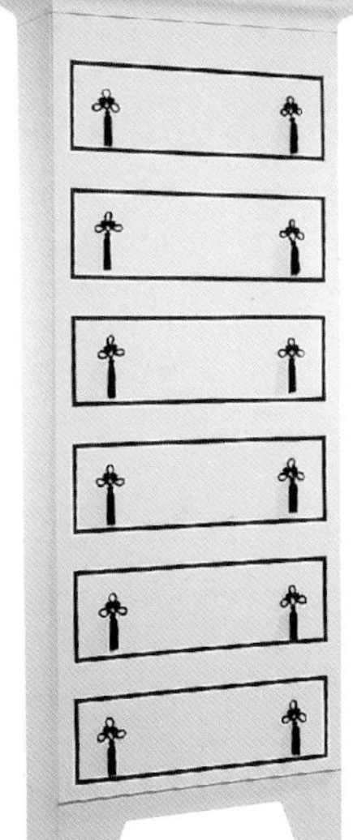

Add feet and plaster cornicing to a basic unit, then attach a single door and paint. Rule on fake drawers with a marker pen, and stick on tassels bought from a haberdashery store.

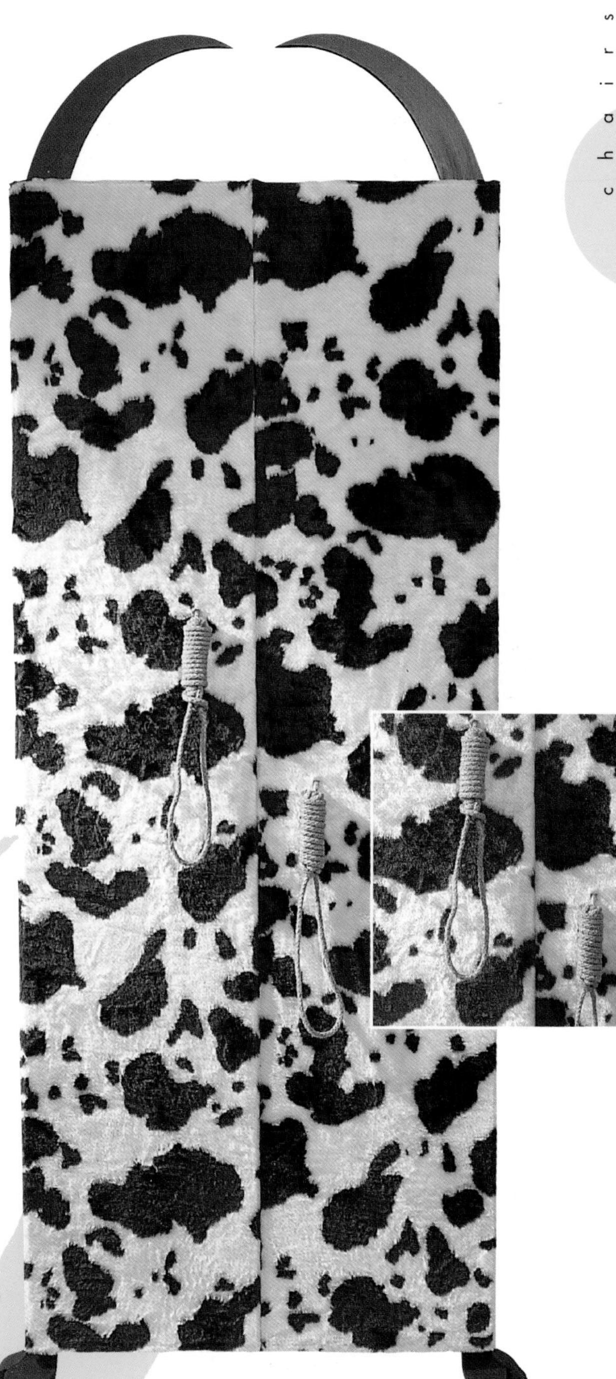

Fake fur was glued to the bookcase doors and the cow motif reinforced with plywood horns and lasso handles.

Corrugated cardboard can be painted with sample-sized pots of paint, then cut to frame the bookshelves to provide a stylish pelmet and surround. The cardboard is simply stuck to the edges of the bookcase with double-sided sticky tape.

You don't need to be an artist to transform a bookcase. Copy one of our designs or try one of your own.

Paint and plaster cornicing are an easy way to add unique style to a cheap unit.

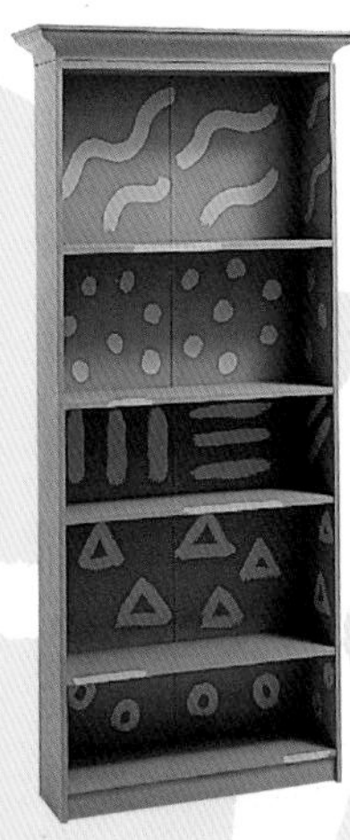

Mounting a bookcase on feet can make an enormous difference to a piece of furniture. Plywood doors transform a humble bookcase into a cupboard. Paint and a gold graphic motif complete the transformation.

Get a buzz out of stencilling on this bee design.

Dramatic black-and-white and tartan ribbons make the original bookcase almost unrecognisable. A length of calico can be turned into a makeshift blind.

Cornicing, feet and doors make the unit look solid. Door handles and gingham fabric give the bookcase a country feel.

A length of muslin dress fabric and pompoms attached to the shelves turn a bookcase into excellent toy storage.

crackle-glaze cupboard

① Apply a coat of primer before painting on the matt emulsion colour you wish to show through your cracks.

② Paint on crackle glaze, haphazardly.

◯ When the glaze has dried, paint over a top colour of matt emulsion and watch the cracks appear.

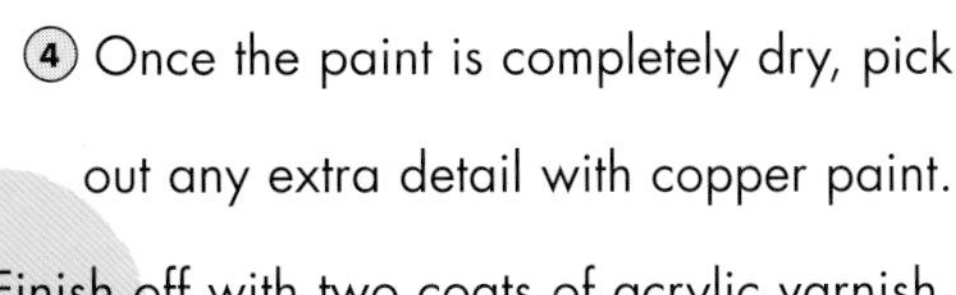

④ Once the paint is completely dry, pick out any extra detail with copper paint. Finish off with two coats of acrylic varnish.

TOP TIPS

- Lay the object flat to minimise the chance of the top coat slipping down the unit as it dries.

TOP TIPS

- For crackle glaze, unlike normal painting, brush the top coat in one direction, not to and fro.
- The thicker you apply the top coat the larger the cracks, but you can only coat the glaze once. If you re-brush the area that you have just applied the top colour to, you will lift the paint off the glaze and the effect will be ruined.
- Protect the result with two coats of acrylic varnish.

in the frame

Even the plainest piece of art benefits from a frame, but picture framers can charge a fortune. It is quite simple to take control of your own artwork and design your frames.

Use clip glass frames or cheap wooden frames as a starting point for your own design. You can use a glue gun to stick twigs, string, leaves or other items to the glass or frame. Normal giftwrap can be used as a backing.

A fun postcard is framed with glued-on toy lizards.

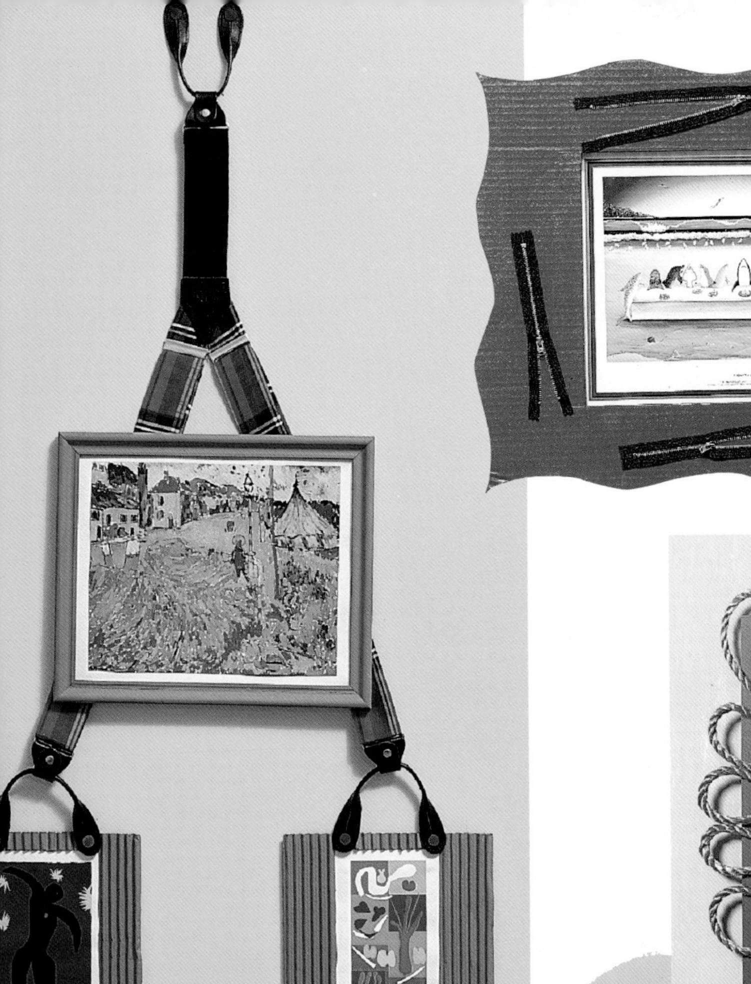

You can use zips, corrugated cardboard, braces or anything you think would be fun.

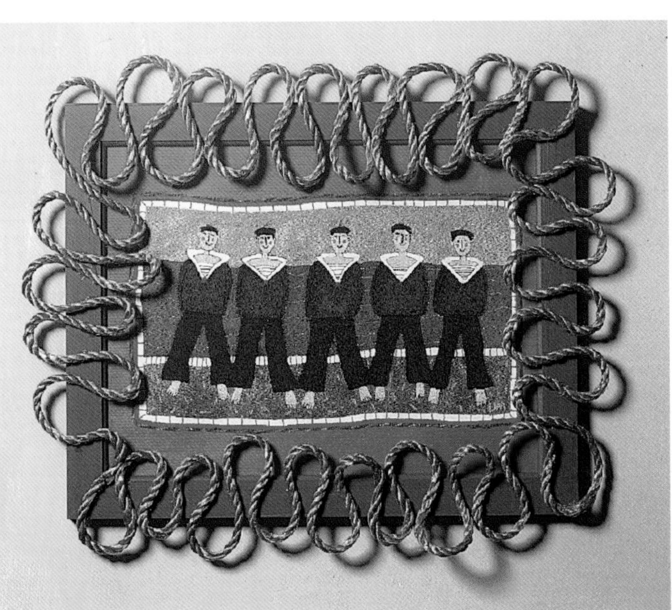

Rope wound loosely and glued to the frame produces a suitably nautical feel.

Attach bay leaves with drawing pins.

the art of laminating

Hiding in the corner of any high-street printers' is the laminating machine. It can be put to better use than sealing conference badges and membership cards. Try this versatile technique for yourself.

A laminate is made of two sheets of clear plastic sealed together with heat. You can take a design made of any thin material like photocopies, ribbon or tissue paper to a print shop and they will laminate it for you.

You can use laminates for placemats, coasters or splashbacks for bathrooms and kitchens. At around £1 for an A4 sheet, laminate is one of the cheapest ways to create something new for your home.

Try using a series of laminates in front of a window. Punch holes, then insert key rings to hold together A4 laminated sheets of tissue paper; hang the completed design from cup hooks.

Torn kitchen foil is laminated, wrapped around an old lampshade and glued in place.

turning the tables

A small table makes an appearance in nearly every home. Give yours a touch of style.

A circular piece of plastic-coated fabric, trimmed with pompoms, can give your table a removable stain-proof surface.

Spray your table with metallic silver paint. Apply a coat of acrylic varnish and sprinkle on glitter and sequins. Allow to dry, then seal the design with two more coats of varnish. Place a sheet of 4mm glass on top for extra protection.

For this wrapped design you first need to cover your table with double-sided sticky tape. Next wind ribbon around the table legs, centre column and top. Protect your table top edge with a circular sheet of 4mm glass.

① Raw wood needs to be lightly sanded and given a coat of acrylic primer before painting.

② Use matt emulsion for a base colour.

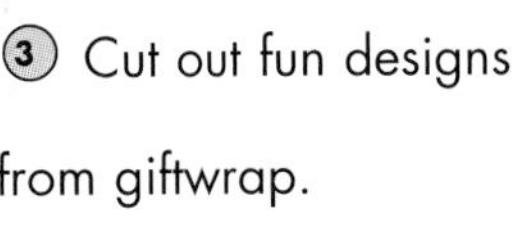

③ Cut out fun designs from giftwrap.

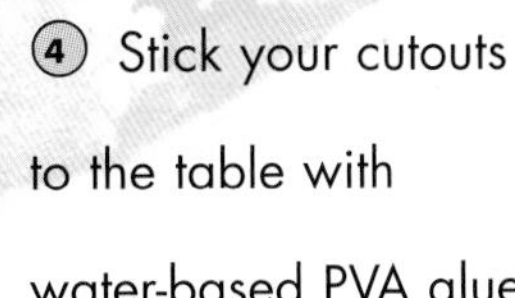

④ Stick your cutouts to the table with water-based PVA glue.

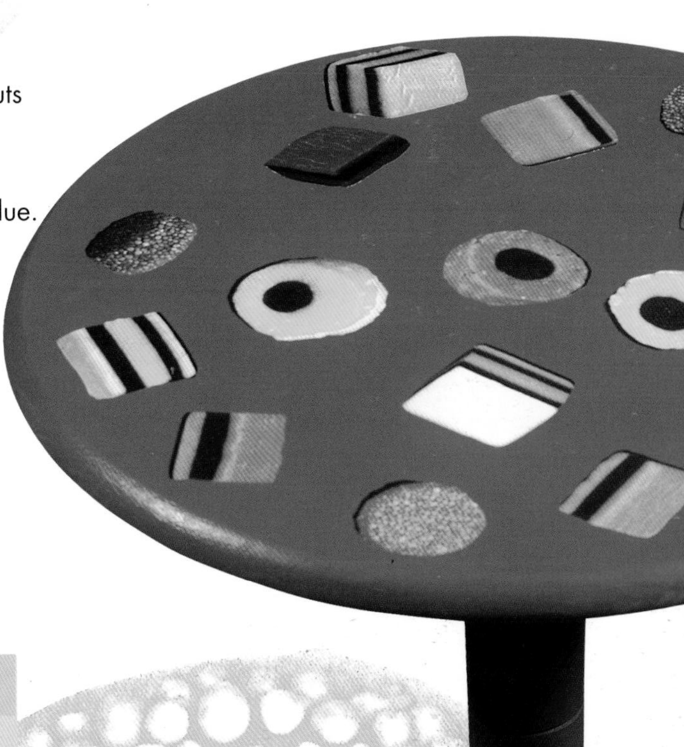

⑤ Satin-finish acrylic varnish will help the design survive more than occasional wear and tear.

TOP TIPS

● The more you use a table, the more coats of varnish you will need to protect the design.

dyeing for a change

A change of colour can make an old piece of fabric look completely new. Dyeing sofa throws, cushion covers, bed linen, curtains and any soft fabric is much cheaper than throwing out old and buying new. It is a solution to be considered when you feel the need for a change.

Fabric dyes come in an enormous range of colours, but bear in mind that, for example, a red dye will not turn a yellow or a green piece of cloth red. The colour on the pack will only be absolutely true for dyeing white fabric.

A tie-dyed throw gives an abstract effect.

Machine-wash dyes are very popular because they are easy to use.

You can also use dye to bring different colours to one piece of fabric. Tie rubber bands around a piece of cloth before dyeing, or tie the cloth itself into a knot. This will prevent dye from reaching all the material, giving you the chance to create more interesting tie-dye effects.

Expert help from dye manufacturers is available; a contact telephone number is listed at the back of the book.

Pouffe or sofa covers can be dyed.

trades

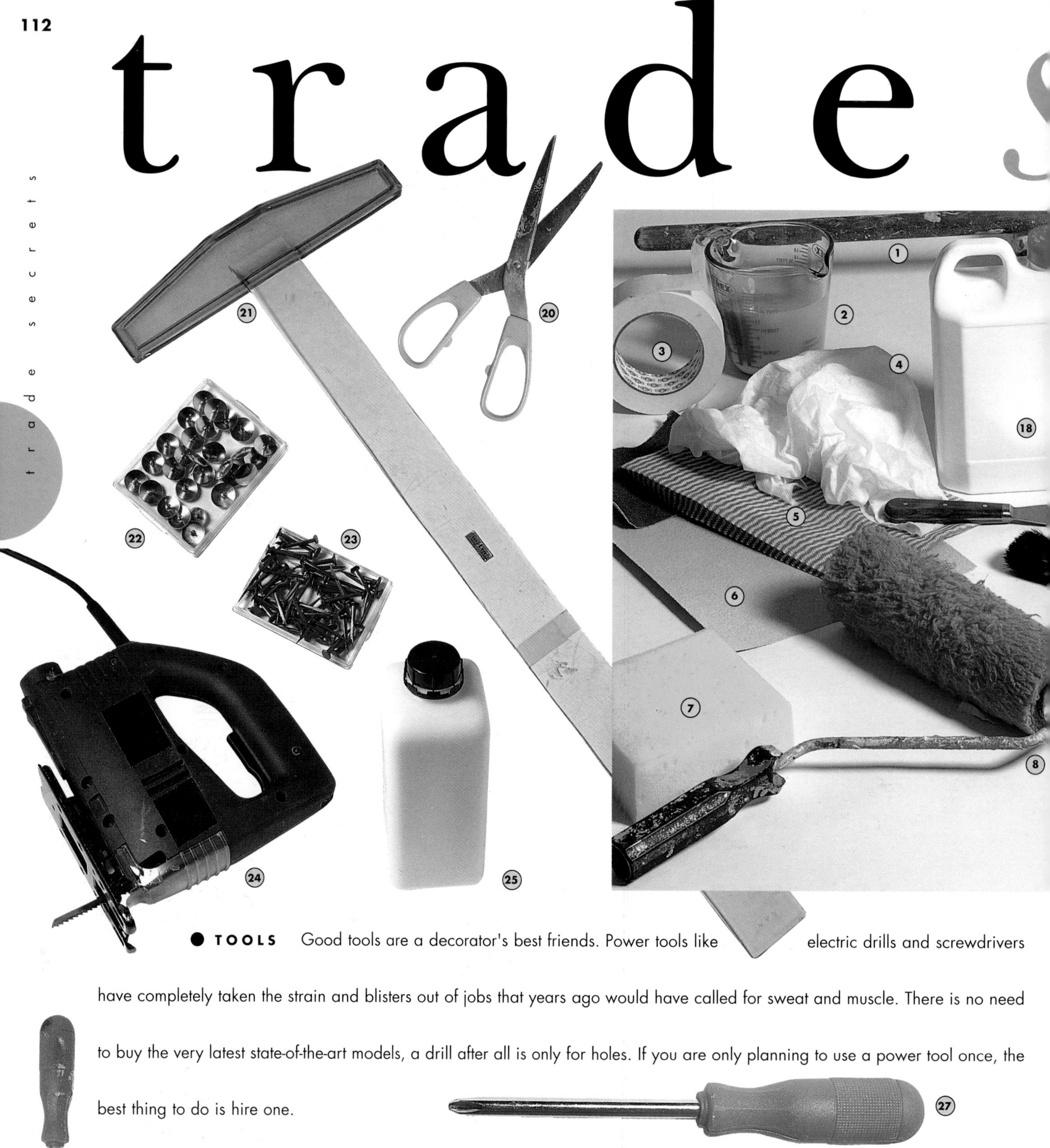

● **TOOLS** Good tools are a decorator's best friends. Power tools like electric drills and screwdrivers have completely taken the strain and blisters out of jobs that years ago would have called for sweat and muscle. There is no need to buy the very latest state-of-the-art models, a drill after all is only for holes. If you are only planning to use a power tool once, the best thing to do is hire one.

27

Be wary of so-called specialist decorating tools. If someone is trying to sell you a decorating sponge for £3 they are ripping you off. Use a £1 bath sponge instead. Top-of-the-range paint brushes are not necessary. One roller, a large and a small brush are all you usually need.

26 28 29

ecrets

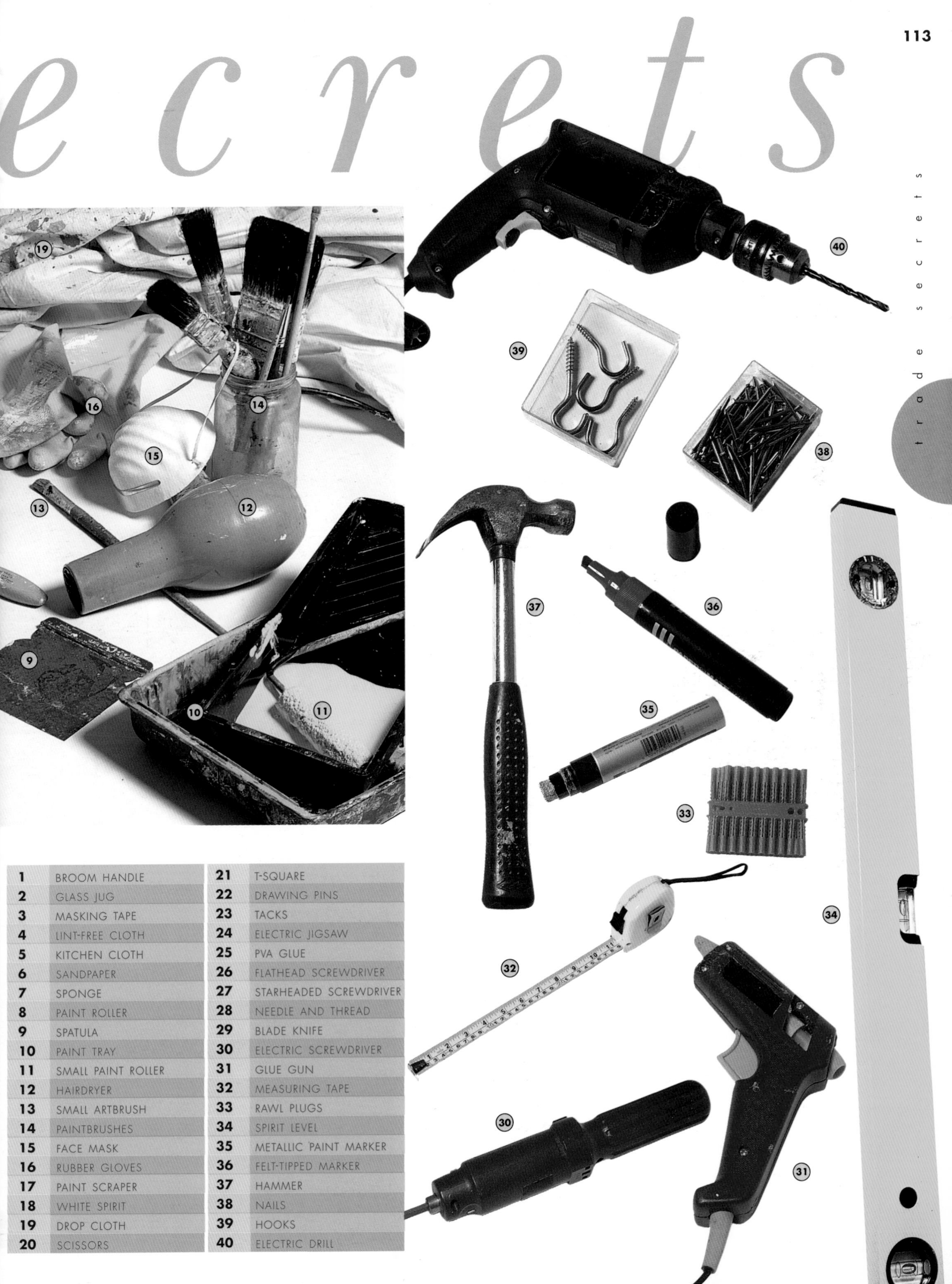

1	BROOM HANDLE	**21**	T-SQUARE
2	GLASS JUG	**22**	DRAWING PINS
3	MASKING TAPE	**23**	TACKS
4	LINT-FREE CLOTH	**24**	ELECTRIC JIGSAW
5	KITCHEN CLOTH	**25**	PVA GLUE
6	SANDPAPER	**26**	FLATHEAD SCREWDRIVER
7	SPONGE	**27**	STARHEADED SCREWDRIVER
8	PAINT ROLLER	**28**	NEEDLE AND THREAD
9	SPATULA	**29**	BLADE KNIFE
10	PAINT TRAY	**30**	ELECTRIC SCREWDRIVER
11	SMALL PAINT ROLLER	**31**	GLUE GUN
12	HAIRDRYER	**32**	MEASURING TAPE
13	SMALL ARTBRUSH	**33**	RAWL PLUGS
14	PAINTBRUSHES	**34**	SPIRIT LEVEL
15	FACE MASK	**35**	METALLIC PAINT MARKER
16	RUBBER GLOVES	**36**	FELT-TIPPED MARKER
17	PAINT SCRAPER	**37**	HAMMER
18	WHITE SPIRIT	**38**	NAILS
19	DROP CLOTH	**39**	HOOKS
20	SCISSORS	**40**	ELECTRIC DRILL

trades

PAINT CHARTS

Item	Paints
BATHROOM WALLS	★
BATH *(OUTSIDE)*	✖ □ ■
CANE FURNITURE	● ■
CEILING	★
CHILDREN'S FURNITURE	● ▮
CHILDREN'S TOYS	○
COFFEE TABLES	● ▮ ■
CORRUGATED PLASTIC	▮ ✖ ■
CUPBOARDS	● ▮ ✖
DINING TABLE	● ▮ ■
DOOR	▮ ✖ □
DOOR HANDLES	▮ ✖ □ ■ ●
FIREPLACE	● ▮ ✖ □
FLOOR - *WOODEN*	● ◆
FLOOR - *CONCRETE*	◆
FLOOR - *VINYL*	● ◆
FRIDGE	▮ ✖ □ ■ ▲
HEARTH	● ▮ ✖ □
KITCHEN WALLS	★ ●
KITCHEN UNIT DOORS	▮ ✖ □
LAMP BASE - *WOODEN*	● ▮ ■
LAMPSHADES	★ ● ■
PICTURE FRAMES	★ ● ▮ ✖ □ ■
PAINTED RUG	●
STAIR HANDRAILS	▮ ✖ □ ■
STAIR TREADS	● ◆
SCREEN	●
SHELF	● ▮ ✖
STENCIL	● ■
SKIRTING BOARD	▮ ✖ □
TOILET SEAT	● ■
WARDROBE	● ▮ ✖ □ ■
WINDOW FRAMES	▮ ✖ □

		PAINT FINISH	PAINT BASE	CLEAN EQUIPMENT WITH
★	MATT EMULSION	*MATT*	WATER	*WATER*
●	MATT EMULSION SEALED WITH ACRYLIC VARNISH	*	WATER	*WATER*
▮	ACRYLIC EGGSHELL	*SLIGHT SHEEN*	WATER	*WATER*
✖	EGGSHELL SATINWOOD	*SLIGHT SHEEN*	OIL	*WHITE SPIRIT*
□	GLOSS	*HIGH SHEEN*	OIL	*WHITE SPIRIT*
◆	FLOOR PAINT	*HIGH SHEEN*	OIL	*WHITE SPIRIT*
■	SPRAY PAINT	*HIGH SHEEN*	OIL	*WHITE SPIRIT*
○	NON-TOXIC	*MATT/SHEEN*	WATER	*WATER*
▲	METAL PRIMER	*MATT/SHEEN*	OIL	*WHITE SPIRIT*

* see varnish chart on page 122

WHERE POSSIBLE USE WATER-BASED PAINTS AND VARNISHES AS THESE ARE MORE ENVIRONMENTALLY FRIENDLY

ecrets

● **PREPARATION** You've bought the paint and you can't wait to slosh it on your walls. Be warned, if you don't prepare properly you will never get a perfect finish and within a year whatever you do will start to look shoddy. You must sand down bumps, fill in cracks. If you are stripping wallpaper, make sure you do bother with those nasty bits that just don't want to come away from the wall. Preparation is a hugely important part of decorating, so don't believe the voice in your head telling you not to bother. Protect flooring and furniture by covering with a drop cloth. A simple bed sheet will not protect your carpet from stray drops of paint as it will seep through, so use a special drop cloth or lay plastic sheeting under a bed sheet. Drop cloths and plastic sheeting are available from decorating shops and it's easier to fold away a cloth than clean paint from your carpet.

● **GLOVES & CLOTHES** Many paints are toxic, and scrubbing even a tiny bit of paint from your fingernails is a boring task, so always wear rubber gloves when painting. Choose a larger size of gloves than you think you need. If you are painting for any length of time your hands will need to breathe and larger paint-splattered gloves are easier to remove. No matter how hard you try or how small an amount of paint you are using, paint will get on your clothes. Paint can tell if you are in your finery and will choose this moment to drip, splatter or smudge. Never paint in clothes you care about. Don't wear woolly socks or jumpers as fluff will stick to paint and varnish. Cotton is the best fabric for decorating in. If you have long hair, always tie it back before painting. Keep your hair out of the paint and the paint out of your hair.

● **FILLING A CRACK** First gouge out the crack with a screwdriver. Making the crack larger might sound bizarre, but you will need to remove bits of plaster that may not look cracked, but are almost certainly damaged. Traditional powder filler, which you mix yourself with water, is far better than ready-mixed filler which is more difficult to sand. Mix the filler with water and then push it firmly into the crack with a spatula. Once the filler is completely dry, sand down the surface with sandpaper.

trades

● **COVERING A WATERMARK** Don't bother eliminating damp patches until you have found where the damp has come from and solve this problem before you do anything else. Allow the area to dry fully, which could take several days. Spray or brush on a stain blocker (available from any decorating shop). When dry, paint the surface back to its original colour.

● **FIXING PEELING PAINT** Peeling usually occurs when moisture has been trapped between the raw surface and the paint layer. Scrape off any loose flakes, sand down to the raw surface, prime and paint.

● **WHERE TO START PAINTING IN A ROOM** Follow the numbers on the sketch when you are painting a room.

1	CEILING
2	WALLS
3	WINDOWS
4	DOORS
5	SKIRTING
6	FLOORS

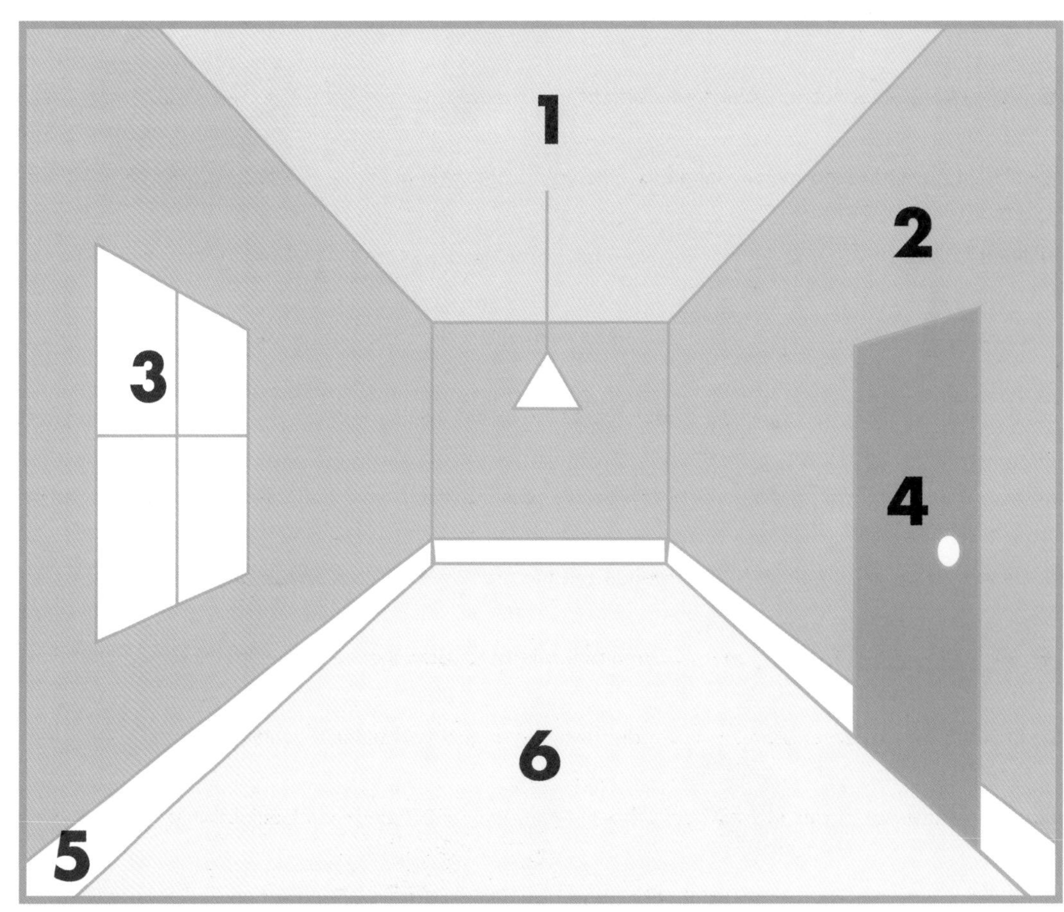

ecrets

● **SANDPAPER AND PREPARING A SURFACE** The most common use of sandpaper is to eliminate bumps and lumps, and to prepare certain surfaces for painting. The type or grade of paper used depends on how much material you need to remove. Rougher paper, graded 40 or 60, is the heavy-duty stuff for big lumps, while the high-grade paper, 100 or 200, is for finer work. You will often need two grades, starting with a low-grade and finishing off with a high-grade paper. Take special care to brush or vacuum up dust after sanding, otherwise it will get in your paint and spoil the finish.

● **PRIMER** Primer is magic stuff, vital if you are planning on painting over raw wood, new plaster or synthetic surfaces like kitchen units. It absorbs resin and helps bond paint to the surface which stops the top coat from flaking. If you miss out a priming coat you are making a serious mistake. You can use acrylic primer underneath oil-based or water-based paint.

● **PAINT** Most tins of paint resist attempts at invasion, so don't resort to gouging at the lid in desperation. Even if you do eventually force a lid open you will never persuade a gouged-out lid to fit properly again. Paint tin lids must be gently levered out with something like a screwdriver; keep moving around the rim of the tin, levering as you go. Always stir paint thoroughly each time you open a tin. This ensures an even blend of colour. When pouring paint into a mixing jug or roller tray be careful not to cover the name of the paint with drips. It's an annoying mistake no one ever makes more than once, but get it wrong and you will be sure to need another pot of that exact shade of green, if only you could remember what it was called. Alternatively, write the name of the paint on the lid of the pot.

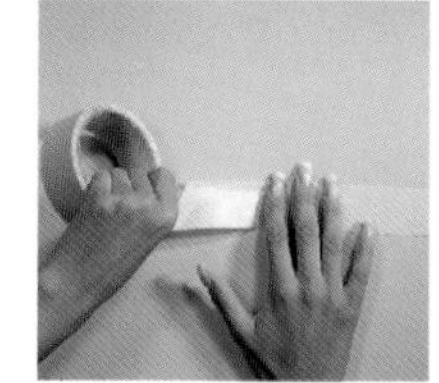

● **MASKING TAPE** You can use masking tape to separate paint colours with a straight edge or to paint stripes on surfaces. As you stick it on, run your finger hard along the side of the tape that will come up against wet paint. This prevents paint from bleeding under the tape and ruining your design. Paint away from masking tape, ensuring that bristles don't go under the tape. The best time to remove masking

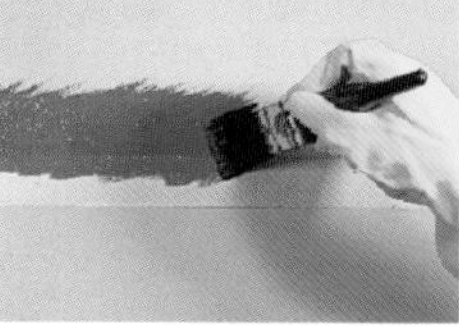

trades

tape is when the paint is half dry. If the paint is completely dry, the tape will tear; if too wet, the paint will run. Peel off the masking tape gently, at an angle away from the wet paint. If you are worried about the masking tape lifting the paint finish you have already painted, rub strips of masking tape against cotton clothing to get rid of some of the stickiness before attaching the not-so-sticky tape to the surface. This will avoid spoiling the paint.

● **PAINTING WITH A BRUSH** Brushes are ideal for small areas and for getting into corners where a roller cannot reach. Avoid the cheapest brushes, which can moult, and choose a medium-priced one with tightly packed bristles. Only buy top-of-the-range if you are going to be decorating on a daily basis. Paint needs to be worked onto a surface, so don't always brush in one direction. For large flat surfaces use a roller where possible.

● **DEBUGGING PAINT** Bugs, hair and dust can ruin the most carefully painted piece of work, so be careful. If you notice something swimming in your paint pot, dip in a brush near the poor little bug and as you remove the brush the insect should come with it. If you only notice a bug once you have applied your paint, use a damp cloth to wipe the area down and start painting all over again. To remove grit from a tin of paint, filter it into a new container using a sieve or an old pair of tights.

● **CLEANING A BRUSH** Like shoes, brushes will take a bit of wearing in, so once you find a brush you love, treat it well. Clean it properly and hang it upside down to dry and store, then it will serve you well for many years. Cleaning up is the worst part of any job and it is tempting to leave dirty paintbrushes until the next day. Resist. The longer you leave paint to dry into bristles, the harder it is to clean. If you don't clean your brushes properly old paint will come back to haunt you as you begin your next project. You can make the job as easy as possible by brushing out any excess paint onto newspaper. If you have been using water-based paint, cleaning is easy, just use warm water. To see if the brush is clean, squeeze out excess water and if it still shows the colour of the paint, try again. For oil-based paints, fill a jam jar with white

spirit to above the level 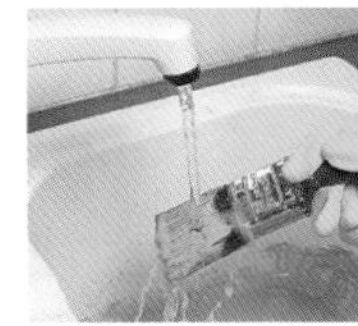 of the bristles, dunk the brush in, use the inside lip of the jar to wipe the excess off the brush then wipe on newspaper. Once you have done this a number of times, pour washing-up liquid right inside the brush and rinse clean with water. If you are going to use  the same oil-based paint within 24 hours, wrap your brush in clingfilm to save cleaning it.

● **PAINTING WITH A ROLLER** Rollers need to be soaked in  paint. Try to get as much paint onto the roller as possible, without having it drip. Don't try to cover too large an area with one application of paint as the roller dries out and the paint will look streaky. Make sure you roll in various directions, not just back and forth. Don't re-roll a wet paint surface as it will lift the paint. If you are painting too quickly and don't come to a complete halt before you lift the roller from the wall it is only too easy to spin the roller, sending tiny specks of paint everywhere. Small rollers are ideal for the doors of kitchen units.

TOP TIPS When painting high ceilings, or floors, try using an old broomstick as an extension for your roller handle.

● **CLEANING A ROLLER** You can use a stick to get rid of excess paint in a roller. Slide the stick down the length of the roller as tightly as you can manage and force it down the length to squeeze out  the paint, preferably over a paint tray. Hold the roller well down under a bath tap to keep splashing to a minimum. Run your fingers through the roller to disperse 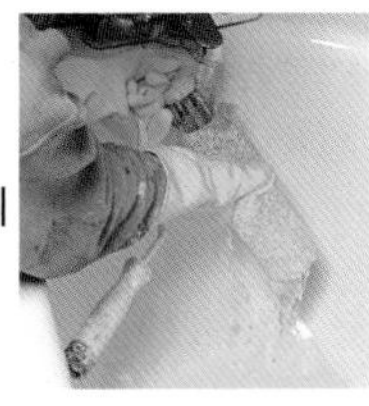 the paint and spin the roller round under the water. Remove the roller sleeve from the handle and wash away all the remaining paint. Rinse thoroughly, place the roller sleeve back on the handle and spin to remove the last traces of water. Remove the roller sleeve and leave it upright to dry. Incidentally, never buy a roller with a non-detachable sleeve, as you will never get it truly clean.

trades

● **HOW TO MIX COLOURWASH** Colourwashes are thinned paints and can be used to break up flat colour. If you want to see a second shade behind a top colour, or want to create a dreamy effect on a wall, you need a colourwash. There's no need to buy one expensively from a shop – make your own. Use a perspex jug or any clear transparent container to mix your wash in. Dilute one part matt emulsion paint with four parts of water. Diluting a paint doesn't affect its colour, it just makes it more transparent, so don't choose a darker or lighter shade than you want because water doesn't affect the colour.

● **HOW TO APPLY COLOURWASH** Once you have a dry coat of matt emulsion, either painted specially or existing in your home, you can slosh on the wash with a brush or rag. For washes it is especially important to keep your brush or rag strokes irregular and heading in all directions. Colourwash dries quickly so speed is of the essence.

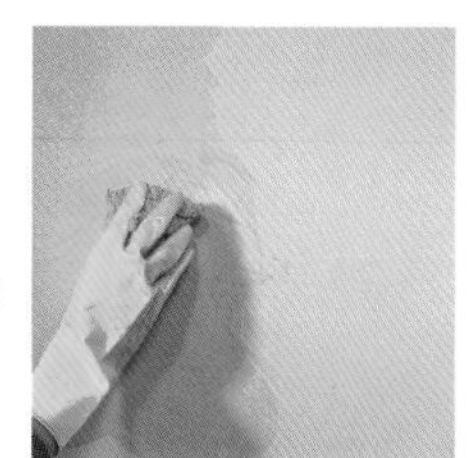

● **PAINTING WITH A BAG** You don't need to limit your painting to rollers and brushes. Try carrier bags, towels, clingfilm, greaseproof paper, anything. Different brush substitutes will give you different paint finishes.

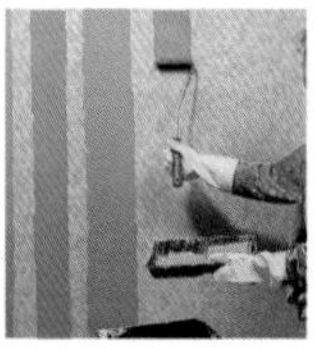

● **PAINTING OVER WALLPAPER** If you can't face stripping off old wallpaper, then you can paint straight over it with matt emulsion paint. This is suitable for both smooth and embossed papers.

● **HAIRDRYER** A hairdryer will speed up the drying time for matt emulsion paint on small painting jobs. This is ideal when stencilling or applying more than one colour to a surface. Hold the hairdryer at least 15cm away from the painted surface or the paint will begin to crack.

● **STORING PAINT** Paint forms a skin when left for more than a month. The best way to stop this from making your paint difficult to use is to store (well-sealed) tins upside down. This way the skin forms on the bottom of the tin, out of harm's way.

ecrets

● **WOODSTAINS** 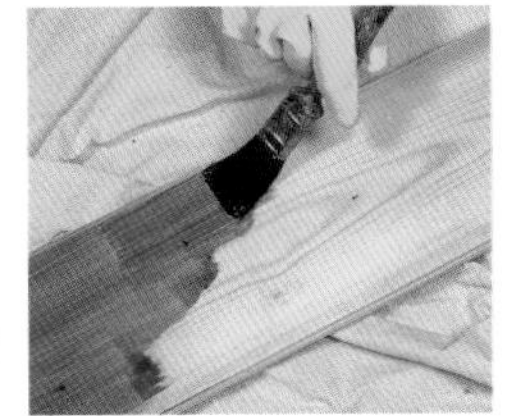 Most affordable wood furniture is made from pine, which has a fresh pale colour. However if you long for the deep rich colour of a wood like mahogany you needn't spend a fortune or worry about rain forest conservation, simply treat with a woodstain. You can match the  colour of any wood you desire with commercially available woodstains. Stir carefully and brush on the stain like a varnish. For colours like this 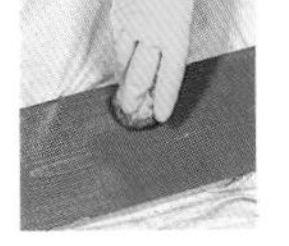 eye-catching blue you will need to mix your own stain. Mix together one part matt emulsion paint to two parts water and stir thoroughly. Apply with a damp rag or brush and after 20–30 seconds use a damp pure cotton kitchen cloth, or old cotton T-shirt to wipe off any excess stain. This allows the grain of the wood to show through the colour. 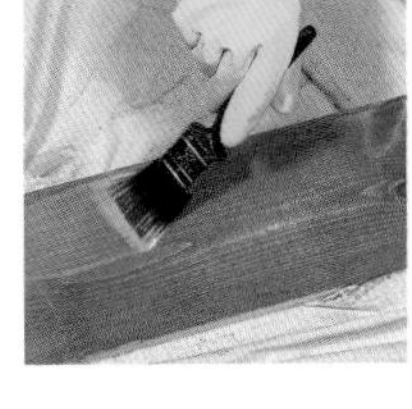 Once the stain is completely dry, seal with acrylic varnish. If you are not sure how deep a stain you want, wipe off any excess even more quickly than you would do normally. You apply many more coats if you want to build up the colour, but you can't undo mistakes without sanding back to bare wood.

● **GLUE** Decorators need PVA glue for sticking down cutout designs, spray glue for holding stencils in position and a glue gun (only £6) for sticking heavier objects. If you use a spray glue, wear a face mask and always keep windows and doors open.

● **HOW TO VARNISH** The first few strokes of paint colour on a blank expanse of wall are always fun. Unfortunately varnish has none of this excitement. It's a dull job, but without it your carefully completed work will chip, fray and wear. Varnishing is always time well spent. Acrylic varnish is streets ahead of other varieties; it is water-based, easy to clean, and dries far faster than polyurethane varnish, so you can apply many more coats in a day. Varnish doesn't necessarily mean shiny. Matt, satin and gloss finishes are available and you should choose the varnish according to the design you want to protect. Never shake a tin of varnish. If you do, air bubbles will form and, once there, they will transfer to your surface. Just stir gently. When you first apply the

trades

surface varnish use criss-cross strokes to work the varnish onto the surface, then switch to continuous strokes, along the line of any grain, before letting each coat dry thoroughly. In between each coat of varnish you will need to sand lightly with a very fine sandpaper, making sure to remove all dust.

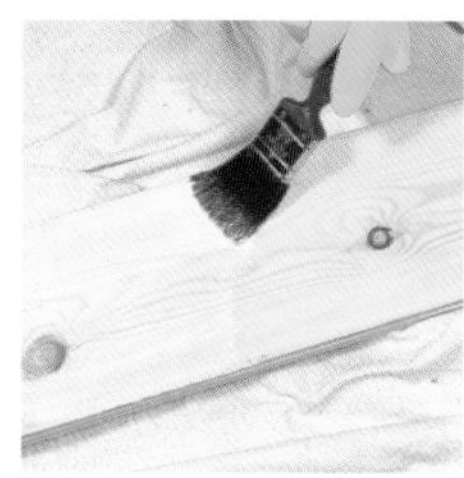

Always check the label for drying times, and be careful of using central heating to speed up the process. A radiator can dry the surface of a wet coat of varnish, but underneath the varnish may still be wet and, like half-dry nail varnish, it will ripple up.

● THE VARNISH CHART

You can judge the number of coats you need according to this table and the amount of wear and tear the object will get.

TO PROTECT	COATS	TO PROTECT	COATS
WALL DESIGN	1	COFFEE TABLE	4
LAMPSHADE	1	HEARTH	4
FIREPLACE	1	CHILDREN'S FURNITURE	4
SCREEN	1	BOOKCASE	4
EXTERIOR OF BATHTUB	2	BATHROOM CUPBOARDS	5
BLANKET BOX	2	KITCHEN CUPBOARDS	5
CHEST OF DRAWERS	2	KITCHEN SPLASHBACK	5 – 8
HANDRAIL	3	WOODEN FLOORING	5 – 10
CHAIRS	3	STAIRS	5 – 10
DINING TABLE	4	PAINTED RUGS OR DESIGNS ON FLOORS	10

The finish you get depends on the type of acrylic varnish that is used.

FLAT ACRYLIC VARNISH *GIVES A MATT FINISH.*

EGGSHELL ACRYLIC VARNISH *GIVES A SLIGHT SHEEN FINISH.*

GLOSS ACRYLIC VARNISH *GIVES A HIGH SHEEN FINISH.*

ecrets

● **STENCILLING** Remountable spray adhesive should be used to 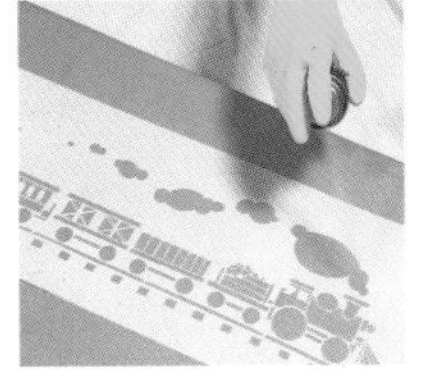 keep the stencil in place. Masking tape may be used but it's not as effective as remountable spray. The spray holds the stencil firmly in place, and you can peel the stencil off and smooth it down again without needing to reach continually for the spray can. Using spray glue stops paint leaking under stencils far better than tape. The best way to stencil is with a synthetic sponge. Use large pieces for big stencils and smaller bits for more delicate work. The secret of successful stencilling is to use as little paint as possible. Work out excess paint onto a piece of card until there is virtually no paint left on the sponge, then dab gently over the stencil.

● **FABRIC** There's no need to spend vast amounts of money on expensive fabrics for soft furnishings like curtains, cushion covers and throws when felt, muslin, dress and lining fabrics are readily available and inexpensive. If you need to make your fabric fire retardant, sprays are available from haberdashery departments.

ENVIRONMENT – BE AWARE! Whenever possible use materials that cause the least amount of damage to the environment. Forget about mahogany, ebony, teak and African walnut; using these in your home is as bad as wearing a real fur coat. Where possible use timber carrying the FSC Trademark – an international symbol that indicates timber and timber products from a well managed source. Water-based and acrylic paints and varnishes are preferable to oil-based ones. Oil-based paints contain solvents in the paints and in the white spirit cleaning solution and are environmentally damaging. Never dispose of solvents down the drain and into the water system. Put them in clearly labelled old paint tins and contact your local authority for their toxic disposal service. Don't bin your old fixtures and fittings, because somebody somewhere can use them. Homeless associations and charities are always looking for old kitchen units, bathroom suites, light fittings, etc. When you're painting, re-use materials as much as possible: buy one pair of tough rubber gloves rather than a pack of lightweight disposable ones; use rags rather than paper towels; buy re-usable rather than disposable items. For more information contact Greenpeace on 0171 865 8100.

shopping *list*

AFRICAN ESCAPE – *Tribal art*
Brian & Susy Reeves
127 Portobello Road
London W11 2DY
t: **0171 221 6650**

HELEN ALLEN – *Furniture designer*
79 Boyton Road
London N8 SAE
t: **0181 340 1990**

ARMITAGE SHANKS LTD
Bathroom fittings suppliers
Armitage
Rugeley
Staffordshire WS15 4BT
t: **01543 490 253**

BHS – *Home furnishings retailers*
BHS Head Office
Marlyebone House
129–137 Marylebone Rd
London
NW1 5QD
t: **0171 262 3288**

J W BOLLOM – *Fake suede and felt fabric suppliers*
316 Old Brompton Road
London
SW5 9JH
t: **0171 370 3252**

BIZ LTD – *Zinc & stainless steel fabricators*
Millmarsh Lane
Brimsdown
Enfield
Middlesex
EN3 7QA
t: **0181 443 3300**

B&Q – *DIY Supercentres*
B&Q Head Office
Portswood House
1 Hampshire Corporate Park
Chandlers Ford
Hampshire
SO53 3YX
t: **01703 256 256**

BY DESIGN – *Handle suppliers*
Studio 702
The Big Peg
120 Vyse Street
Birmingham
B18 6NF
t: **0121 604 3300**

SOPHIE CHANDLER
Alternative lighting & furniture
Please call for stockists only
t: **0171 582 2676**

SARAH CLARKE – *Seamstress*
115 Mandrake Road
London SW17 SPX
t: **0181 672 7189**

CRAIG & ROSE PLC
Varnish and paint suppliers
172 Leith Walk
Edinburgh
EH6 5EB
t: **0131 554 1131**

CROWN – *Paint and Lincrusta wallpaper suppliers*
PO Box 37 Crown House
Hollins Road
Darwen
Lancashire BB3 OBG
t: **01254 704 951**

DO IT ALL LTD
For list of stores ring head office on
t: **01384 456456**

DULUX – *Paint suppliers*
Wexham Rd
Slough
Berkshire
SL2 5DS
t: **01753 550 000**

DYLON INTERNATIONAL LTD
Fabric dye suppliers
Worsley Bridge Road
Lower Sydenham
London
SE26 5HD
t: **0181 663 4296**

EDGAR UDNEY & CO LTD
Mosaic suppliers
314 Balham High Road
London
SW17 7AA
t: **0181 767 8181**
Ask for samples as catalogues show incorrect colours

ELEPHANT PLC
Furniture and accessories
94 Tottenham Court Road
London W1P 9HE
t: **0171 813 2092**

FIRED EARTH PLC – *Tile suppliers*
Call the head office on
01295 812 088 *for suppliers*

GET PLASTERED
Mail order plaster kit and casts supplier
t: **0378 812 896**

shopping *list*

HABITAT – *Furniture retailer*
The Heals Building
196 Tottenham Court Road
London W1P 9 LD
t: **0171 255 2545**

HOMEBASE
For list of stores ring head office on
t: **0181 784 7200**

LINZI HODGES
Decorative glass & metal designer
6 Maesgwynsryn
Gwespyr
Flintshire North Wales
CH8 9LE
t: **0839 419 834** (pager)

HUMBROL LTD
Spray paint suppliers
Marfleet
Hull HU9 5NE
t: **01482 701 191**

IKEA LTD – *Furniture store*
255 North Circular Road
London NW10 OJQ
t: **0181 233 2300**

JOHN LEWIS *Department stores*
For nearest store call Oxford Street
t: **0171 629 7711**

PENNY KENNEDY DESIGN
Giftwrap suppliers
Unit One
Jamestown Business Park
Jamestown
Dunbartonshire G83 8BZ
t: **01389 755 516**

LAKELAND PLASTICS LTD
Mail order kitchen and houseware products
Alexandra Buildings
Windermere
Cumbria
LA23 1BQ
t: **01539 488100**

LEYLAND PAINT CO.
Builders' and decorators' merchants
371–373 Edgware Road
London
W2 1BS
t: **0171 723 8048**

LONDON GRAPHIC CENTRE
Mail order artist and graphic materials suppliers
16–18 Shelton Street
London
WC2H 9JJ
t: **0171 240 0095**

NATALIE MAGEE
Glass and 3D designer
29 Warwick Drive
Cheshunt
Waltham Cross
Herts
EN8 OBN
t: **01992 628 116**
t: **01772 885 782**

MFI – *Furniture centres*
Southon House
333 The Hyde
Edgware Rd
Colindale
London NW9 6TD
t: **0181 200 8000**

NU-LINE – *Builders' and decorators' merchants*
315 Westbourne Park Road
London W11 1EF
t: **0171 727 7748**

PAPERCHASE
mail order stationery and paper retailer
For list of stores ring head office on
t: **0171 636 1333**

PENTONVILLE RUBBER CO. LTD
Foam suppliers
104 Pentonville Road
London N1 9JB
t: **0171 837 4582**

THE PIER RETAIL LTD
Homestore
For list of stores ring head office on
t: **01235 821088**

PLASTERWORKS
Plastercast suppliers
38 Cross Street
Islington
London NW1 2BG
t: **0171 226 5355**

PLASTI-KOTE LTD
Spray paint suppliers
London Road Industrial Estate
Sawston
Cambridge CB2 4TP
t: **01223 836 400**

PURVES & PURVES
Furniture and accessory retailer
80–83 Tottenham Court Road
London W1 9HD
t: **0171 580 8223**

shopping *list*

RJ'S – *Homestore*
209 Tottenham Court Road
London W1P 9AF
t: **0171 637 7474**

LYNNE ROBINSON & RICHARD LOWTHER – *Murals & made-to-order stencils*
29 rue de l'Homme de Bois
14600 Honfleur
France
t: **00 33 31894441**

SANTORO GRAPHICS LTD
Giftwrap designs
The Old Bank House
342–344 London Road
Cricket Green
Mitcham
Surrey
CR4 3ND
t: **0181 640 9777**

SIGNS & DESIGNS
in wood, glass & stone
David Mackaey
Thrumster Cottage Wick
Caithness
KW1 5TX
Scotland
t: **01955 651248**

SPECIALIST CRAFTS LTD
Mail order art & craft materials
PO Box 247
Leicester LE1 9QS
t: **0116 251 0405**

STENCIL LIBRARY
Mail order stencil supplier
Stocksford Hall
Stocksford
Northumberland
NE 43 7TN
t: **01661 844 844**

SHIRES – *Bathroom fittings suppliers*
Beckside Road
Bradford
West Yorkshire BD7 2 JE
t: **01274 521199**

CLARE THATCHER
Made-to-order decorative lighting
44 Seymour Rd
Chingford
London E4 7LS
By appointment only.
t: **0181 524 0912**

TRUMPET DESIGN
Sue Williams Greetings card designs
Flat 1
6 Pond Road
Blackheath
London SE3 9JL
t: **0181 297 8966**

THE WATER MONOPOLY
Bathrooms
16–18 Lonsdale Road
London NW6 6RD
t: **0171 624 2636**

WEST TEN GLASS
485 Latimer Road
London
W10 6RD
t: **0181 969 5682**

WORLD'S END TILES & FLOORING
Ceramic tile manufactures
Railway Goods Yard
Silverthorne Road
London
SW8 3HE
t: **0171 720 8358**

WICKES BUILDING SUPPLIERS
DIY Superstore
Boston Road
Hanwell
London
W7 3SA
t: **0181 567 6588**

ROBERT WYATT – *Lampshades*
13 The Shrubbery
Grosvenor Road
Wanstead
London
E11 2EL
t: **0181 530 6891**

index

acknowledgements

Authors' *Acknowledgements*

Extra special thanks to...

Colin Poole for his patience, wit and Lassie Come Home impressions; Annabelle Poole for keeping Colin in line; Kes James for the use of the expression 'nightmare'; Jeremy Gordon for the introduction to the BBC and everything else; Anthea Morton-Saner for believing in the book; Daisy Goodwin for giving me new horizons; Wesley Bolton for turning my drawings into wonderful realities; Judith Burton for being the best there is; Kathleen Duffy for the encouragement; Debbie Semon for lending an ear; Katrina Sandlin for being as big as they come.

Without whom...

Andy Batt & Martin, Todd Bolton, Martin Butler, Audrey Carden, John Duckworth, Greg Demosthenous, Keith Fuller, Frank Farci, Alan Firman, Louise Holgate, Molly Johnson, Dominic Luscombe, Gail MacGregor, Michael Penford, Scott Phillips, Alison Pearce, Tony Randel, Seiriol Tomos, Rikki Tamrat, Caroline Tyler, Barbara Vidal-Hall.

Into their homes...

Diane & Andrew Holmes, Patsy Youngstein, Sascha O'Hagan, Sam Morse, Kate & Kristan Stone, Rachel & Izzy Selly, Karen McGill, Fiona Cole, Tonia Nagel, Russel Denton, Louise & Tom Walsh, Jaimie & Louise, Cláire Mulley, Susan Campbell, Brian & Emma Wares.

Thanks to...

Pamela Anderson, Paula Bridges, Katy Eachus, Lorna Frame, Kaye Godleman, Asif Hasan, Elaine Hill, Diana Henry, Tommy & Jaqui Hopkins, Sascha Jeffrey, Janine Josman, Anvar Khan, Ariane Koek, Geraldine McClelland, Trisha O'Leary, B. Orlando; Pat, John, Pauline and everyone at Crispins; Richard Peskin, Patricia Rutherford, Joey Searle, Margeurite Smith, S. Tripoda, Helen Williams of Stencil Library, Simon Morris at Texas/Homebase; Colin Mitchell Rose at Craig & Rose; Leyland Paints – Edgware Road; Evelyn Strout at John Lewis; William at Ikea; Purves & Purves, Samantha at the Water Monopoly; David Mackay of Signs & Designs; Dylon; Plasterworks; Lakeland Plastics; Jonathon Pellegrini.

Goods supplied by...

African Escape: page 57 *(tribal art)*; Stencil Library: pages 19 *(zebra)*, 22 *(rug border)*, 28 *(tiles)*, 39 *(mosaic)*, 48 *(leaf)*, 55 *(tiles)*, 64 *(floor tile)*, 79 *(hearth & column)*, 80 *(fleur de lys)*, 92 *(laurel wreath)*, 96 *(flying pigs)*, 102 *(bees)*, 123 *(train)*; Lynne Robinson & Richard Lowther: page 23 from Stencilling Book; Texas/Homebase Kitchens: pages 38 & 48; Water Monopoly: inspiration for pages 60 & 61; Sophie Chandler: page 19 *(bottle light)*; Helen Allen: page 24 *(pouffe)*; Robert Wyatt: page 13 *(lamp)*; Purves & Purves: page 13 *(sofas)*; Elephant: page 13 *(cushions, coffee table and accessories)*; Linzi Hodges: page 13 *(glass bottles)*; Sue Magee: page 13 *(glass dish)*; Ikea: page 13 *(rug)*; Plasterworks: page 18 *(head)*; Santoro Design: pages 43, 87, 106, 107, 109 *(giftwrap)*; Penny Kennedy Design: pages 30,31 *(giftwrap)*; Trumpet Design: page 57 *(card)*; Paperchase: pages 87, 106, 107 *(giftwraps)*; John Lewis: page 84 (glass); David Mackay: page 105 *(sailor giftwrap)*; Dylon dyes were used throughout the book. The varnishes and floor paints used throughout this book were supplied by Craig & Rose.

See Shopping List for relevant addresses and telephone numbers.

Photographs

All the following photographs by Colin Poole:

Pages 13, 14, 15, 16, 17, 18, 19, 20, 21, 22, 23, 24, 25, 28, 34, 35, 36, 38, 39, 40, 41, 42, 43, 44, 45, 46, 47, 48, 49, 50, 51, 52, 53, 55, 59, 64, 65, 66, 68, 69, 70, 71, 72, 73, 74, 75, 78, 80, 81, 82, 83, 84, 85, 86, 87, 88, 89, 90, 91, 92, 93, 97, 103, 105, 107, 110. © 1996 Anne McKevitt.

Pages 2, 3, 4, 5, 6, 7, 10, 11, 12, 29, 30, 31, 56, 57, 62, 63, 67, 76, 77, 94, 95, 98, 99, 100, 101, 102, 106, 107, 108, 109, 114, 115, 116, 117, 118, 119, 120, 121. © 1996 Anne McKevitt & Shelley Warrington.

Pages 32, 33, 79, 96, 104, 111, 112, 113. © 1996 Shelley Warrington.

Additional photography of Anne McKevitt's designs:

Capitol Photographs: pages; 36, 44 *(after)*, 55, 69, 85.
Chris Wood: pages 20, 21 *(before)*, 66 *(before)*, 68, 88 *(before & after)*, 89 *(before)*.
Kitchens, Bedrooms & Bathrooms/Steve Hawkins: page 85 *(main shot)*.

The publishers wish to thank the photographers and organisations for their kind permission to reproduce the following photographs in this book:

Belle Magazine/Sharrin Rees: pages 8–9; *Vogue Living*/Simon Kenny: page 13 above; Antoine Bootz *(designer Dana Nicholson)* pages 26-27; Lavinia Press: page 27 above and below; *World of Interiors*/Jonathan Lovekin: page 27 centre; Jerome Darblay *(Jean-Jacques Ory)*: page 37; La Casa de Marie Claire/Edouardo Munoz: page 54; Elizabeth Whiting & Associates/Mark Luscombe-Whyte: page 58; Robert Harding Picture Library/*Country Homes & Interiors* IPC Magazines/Polly Wreford: pages 60–61.